Stuxnet to Sunburst

STUXNET TO SUNBURST

20 Years of Digital Exploitation and Cyber Warfare

Andrew Jenkinson

CRC Press
Taylor & Francis Group
Boca Raton London New York

CRC Press is an imprint of the
Taylor & Francis Group, an **informa** business

First edition published 2022
by CRC Press
6000 Broken Sound Parkway NW, Suite 300, Boca Raton, FL 33487-2742

and by CRC Press
2 Park Square, Milton Park, Abingdon, Oxon, OX14 4RN

© 2022 Taylor & Francis Group, LLC

CRC Press is an imprint of Taylor & Francis Group, LLC

The right of Andrew Jenkinson to be identified as author of this work has been asserted by him in accordance with sections 77 and 78 of the Copyright, Designs and Patents Act 1988.

Reasonable efforts have been made to publish reliable data and information, but the author and publisher cannot assume responsibility for the validity of all materials or the consequences of their use. The authors and publishers have attempted to trace the copyright holders of all material reproduced in this publication and apologize to copyright holders if permission to publish in this form has not been obtained. If any copyright material has not been acknowledged please write and let us know so we may rectify in any future reprint.

Except as permitted under U.S. Copyright Law, no part of this book may be reprinted, reproduced, transmitted, or utilized in any form by any electronic, mechanical, or other means, now known or hereafter invented, including photocopying, microfilming, and recording, or in any information storage or retrieval system, without written permission from the publishers.

For permission to photocopy or use material electronically from this work, access www.copyright. com or contact the Copyright Clearance Center, Inc. (CCC), 222 Rosewood Drive, Danvers, MA 01923, 978-750-8400. For works that are not available on CCC please contact mpkbookspermissions@tandf.co.uk

Trademark notice: Product or corporate names may be trademarks or registered trademarks and are used only for identification and explanation without intent to infringe.

ISBN: 978-1-032-06849-7 (hbk)
ISBN: 978-1-032-06850-3 (pbk)
ISBN: 978-1-003-20414-5 (ebk)

DOI: 10.1201/9781003204145

Typeset in Caslon
by SPi Technologies India Pvt Ltd (Straive)

Contents

PREFACE		vii
ABOUT THE AUTHOR		xi
CHAPTER 1	THE WORLDWIDE EXPLOSION OF PERSONAL COMPUTERS AND THE AFTERTHOUGHT THAT IS SECURITY	1
CHAPTER 2	9/11 AND THE CREATION OF MASS DATA COLLECTION IN THE NAME OF SECURITY...	7
CHAPTER 3	PRISM, PROJECT AURORA, AND EARLY DIGITAL OFFENSIVE CAPABILITY	13
CHAPTER 4	STUXNET TO ZERO DAYS	19
CHAPTER 5	HUSH PUPPIES, FLYING PIGS, GROWING TENSIONS, AND EASTER EGGS	27
CHAPTER 6	ROOT CAUSE ANALYSIS, ASTON MARTINS AND CONCORDE	37
CHAPTER 7	THE OFFICE OF PERSONNEL MANAGEMENT AND EQUIFAX BREACHES	45
CHAPTER 8	MARRIOTT AND CYBER INSURANCE: A FRAGILE PROP	53
CHAPTER 9	FROM BOOM TO BUST, OR FROM $3 BILLION FLOATATION TO $1 SALE IN 18 MONTHS	59

VI CONTENTS

Chapter 10	Did Someone Say Critical National Infrastructure and Nuclear Power	65
Chapter 11	Cyberattack Fatigue	75
Chapter 12	Not Secure, the Vatican and Healthcare	83
Chapter 13	Australia's Frustration with China and Assisting the FBI	91
Chapter 14	Blackbaud and Third-Party Trust	99
Chapter 15	Stuxnet to Sunburst	105
Chapter 16	www.avsvmcloud(.)com (SolarWinds Attack) the Modus Operandi for Attacks Since Stuxnet	111
Chapter 17	The TAO, Quantum Insert, and Own Goals	121
Chapter 18	The COVID-19 Breaches	129
Chapter 19	Should We Be Concerned or Worried? Our Government and Agencies Have Got This	137
Chapter 20	Making the Matter Far Worse (IoT and 5G)	143
Chapter 21	NSA Obsolete TLS Protocols	151
Chapter 22	What Does the Future Hold? By Asking Better Questions, We Will Get Better Answers and Take Better Action	161
Index		169

Preface

During the 20th century, counterintelligence was aimed at having eyes and ears focused on gathering as much information as possible and from as diverse a group as possible. What could possibly be more powerful than knowing what your enemy was thinking or indeed doing? It became quite normal for spies, and then double agents, to share information and intelligence, often with a twist. It could be considered what we term today as fake news. Swapping notes and being caught in 'honey pot' traps of prostitution and bundles of cash was a regular occurrence. It was deemed a necessary evil to play dirty tactics in any way shape or form to gain insight and intelligence that could be used for an advantage over one's adversaries. Regular killings and mysterious accidents occurred. It was relived throughout the 1960s and 1970s mildly in many cinema outings where films such as James Bond and Tinker Tailor Soldier Spy retold and shared the challenges of MI5 and MI6 in the 1950s and 1960s and many more. It was beyond the realm of reality to most people's beliefs or even imagination. Yet, there were tens of thousands, moving to hundreds of thousands of operatives deployed in various agencies around the world predominantly the US, UK, Germany, Russia, and more latterly China, among others.

On 14 August 1941, Five Eyes was formed which was an alliance of five major, English speaking intelligence agencies and countries.

PREFACE

These were namely Australia, Canada, New Zealand, the UK, and the USA. They all signed up to become party to a UK/US agreement and a treaty for joint intelligence cooperation and sharing of secretive intelligence. It was some decades later that the US started encryption and digital eavesdropping that would bring this treaty into question by undermining the parties involved. The US planted digital eavesdropping capabilities unbeknown to their partners at the time (see Chapter Crypto AG/OMNISEC). Fast forward to the 1990s when a program, code-named ECHELON, was disclosed that triggered a major debate in the European Parliament. The ECHELEON surveillance system was originally developed to monitor communications between the former Soviet Union and the Eastern Bloc and is considered the forerunner to many other global monitoring global communications.

Five Eyes went further and wanted to monitor the explosion of the newly created Tim Burners-Lee developed World Wide Web (WWW) in the early 1990s whilst he was working at the organisation Europeene pour la Recherche Nucleaire (CERN). The first website was info@cern.ch and was originally conceived and developed to meet the demand for automated information sharing between scientists in universities and institutes around the world. In the mid to late 1990s and into the new decade, a major shift to digital, cyber counterintelligence was like a digital arms race and was being perfected, and indeed taught. With both Presidential and Parliamentary support, programs were pushed through and signed off. The massive focus on this area and capability was never more prevalent than post the terrorist attacks on the World Trade Center towers of 9/11/2001. Billions of US$s was ploughed into the development of Cyber intelligence in the US along with mass digital surveillance on programs such as PRISM, XKEYSCORE, and QUANTUM INSERT and many more. No longer did the Western world need to rely upon intelligence gathered via secretive, clandestine conversations and slipped notes. All that was now required was an email address, an Internet Protocol (IP) Address, or an internet connection…

The transition from physical to digital surveillance was made all too easy coupled with intelligence gathering and became irresistible and intoxicating for the agencies and governments. What started out post 9/11 as the digital eavesdropping of international communications between various, listed known adversary countries, identified individuals and the US, quickly became rolled out globally and it

PREFACE

IX

no longer mattered who it was. Data would be and was collected on everyone including Five Eyes partners and governments en masse.

Revelations by Edward Snowdon in 2013 confirmed that the Five Eyes, led very much by the US, was in fact a supranational intelligence organisation that did not always answer to the laws of its own governments and countries. This enabled the circumvention of what was deemed, by the agencies at least, to be otherwise restrictive. The agencies effectively did what they wanted, to whom they wanted. They could take over command and control of PCs and laptops, gain access to Prime Minister's most intimate details, and effectively determine elections by their, or other's infiltration. For a decade or so, they had full reign and control. However, as time passed, the very backdoors they developed and that they encouraged (forced) many major tech and telco firms to build in for their own use, became poorly kept secrets and then known adopted globally by our adversaries. Such methods became the Modus Operandi for other countries in the form of State Nations and cybercriminals. Ultimately, the monster was turned on its creator, and with devastating effect. The agencies forged ahead with their digital, offensive programs and never thought once to stop and consider the consequences of their actions. They also, by way of their inactions, actively discouraged controls of encryption and security, they were far too busy manipulating it. Why would they want to make it harder for themselves and easier for everyone else to gain visibility? Their investment and ownership in various social media companies and global encryption corporates showed their goal and end game plan, that of full control.

This book shares just some of the sequence of these events in more detail, what happened, what is happening, including early insight into the recent SolarWinds massive breach, a breach that has dire consequences and is being termed as a 'Grave concern' by the US government. It also looks at what will happen if we allow things to remain unchanged and continue playing the poor little old me card. Our governments created the challenges we face today, we simply cannot delay remediation. Whilst handfuls of individuals and companies continue making substantial profits within the security sector, themselves pushing security whilst many maintain not being secure themselves. Immaterial of the market forces and trends, cyberattacks, losses, and costs will hit $6 trillion by the end of 2021 making it the world's third largest economy behind China and the US. Unless things are

PREFACE

radically addressed, China will catch up and equal the US's GDP, and already has the goal to become the world's No. 1 economy and surpass it. China have undoubtedly played the long game and, unless we address and remediate the massive vulnerabilities caused by our own agencies' self-inflicted vulnerabilities, China may well see their efforts and goals achieved sooner rather than later.

The release on 5 January 2021 by the NSA of their cybersecurity paper and information sheets detailing how to detect and fix out-of-date encryption protocol implementations confirms what we have been saying for a considerable time. Networks and systems using deprecated Transport Layer Security (TLS) or Secure Sockets Layer (SSL) for traffic sessions risk sensitive data exposure and decryption, no matter who is looking. Reading between the lines for just a moment, it makes for an interesting shift by the NSA, and their associated agencies. All agencies have been known to have perfected and manipulated vulnerabilities of TLS/SSL to gain access themselves through their programs such as QUANTUM INSERT, FLYING PIGS, HUSH PUPPY, and PRISM over the last 20 years. Can we hope this: Reset, Ctrl, Alt, Del moment is a milestone, and our lobbying has started to finally pay off. What we need now is the NSA to acknowledge the same issues of digital certificates and encrypted keys that make up Public Key Infrastructure (PKI) that has been used to manipulate every company, cause service outages and were originally used in cyberattacks against Iranian Nuclear facilities and more latterly, the US government via the SolarWinds breach? We continue to offer our support and technical capability and urge governments and the public to demand security by design, not an afterthought.

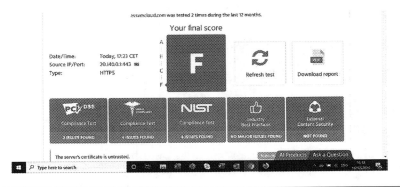

Figure 0.1 Screenshot taken during last year's SolarWinds breach in December; it was discovered that Domain Admin Access was gained and the domain that stood up was avsvmcloud.com.

About the Author

Andrew Jenkinson is a senior and seasoned innovative executive with over 30 years' experience as a hands-on lateral thinking CEO coach and leader. A 'big deal' business accelerator and thinker, Andy has created and been responsible for delivering over £100M of projects within the Cyber, Technical, Risk and Compliance markets with some of the world's largest leading organisations. An inspirational leader and lateral thinker, Andy has a demonstrable track record of large-scale technical delivery and management within Professional Services, Managed Services, and Financial Services environments. Andy has extensive experience of working at C-Level and is well known around the world for his strong business leadership, integrity, acumen, development, and change management.

Andy's first book, 2021, titled '*Stuxnet to Sunburst, 20 years of digital exploitation and cyber warfare*' is a candid, practitioners' view and experience of how digital warfare over the last 20 years has shaped our world. It uncovers many unknown facts that the public have been totally unaware of, until now. Andy was one of the first, and possibly the only person, to uncover the plethora of insecure SolarWinds domains that were responsible for and the root cause of the initial infiltration (Sunburst). Andy's research was presented to the US Senate Intelligence Committee overseeing the SolarWinds breach earlier this year.

ABOUT THE AUTHOR

Andy has just finished writing a second book on his experience and in-depth research of over 1000 companies over the last few years, all of whom have been victims of cyber and ransomware attacks. The book is titled *"Ransomware and Cyberwar, the global economic shift."*

Andy has an uncanny ability to see things in straightforward, no nonsense manner and translate them into easily digestible chunks that can be addressed and remediated. His recall and real examples of cyber and ransomware attacks provide insights and why attacks occur, and more importantly, how to prevent them.

Last year Andy was featured in The Catholic News Agency article on his research of The Vatican breach as he unravelled and assisted The Vatican by identifying that 82 out of their 85 domains, many capturing PII data and payments, were Not Secure. With 1.2 billion followers online, particularly during Covid-19 lockdowns, Andy may have uncovered the root cause for the world's single largest online digital PII data breach to date.

1

THE WORLDWIDE EXPLOSION OF PERSONAL COMPUTERS AND THE AFTERTHOUGHT THAT IS SECURITY

In the 1970s, the personal computer market went through an incredible explosion which began with the microcomputer. The personal computer was originally only intended for interactive, individual use as opposed to the existing, but relatively new, mainframe computers that IBM had developed and cornered the market since its inception on 16 June 1911. Computers had seen a steady growth and companies quickly realised the benefits of using computers to undertake regular, daily tasks. As with every single development of computing through the ages, right up to today's Quantum Computers, no one considered or thought or prioritised security, it was all about functionality: It was very much a case of 'don't worry, we can try to secure it later.' Billions of IOT devices confirm this.

This was very much the case when personal computers were first introduced. The first shipment and batch of personal computers went out without any security whatsoever. Sometime thereafter, an executive considered security and so the next batches went out with a security code, they all went out with the same code, so much for security. IoT devices follow a similar situation today. Security has always played second fiddle to functionality in most walks of life, that is the case in technology. As the saying goes, it is easier to be the first and gain market share, than it is to be the best and stay there. Security and breaches can be dealt with by insurers and others and can be dismissed. It has almost become a 'cost of doing businesses.' Until regulators and governance is stricter and demands basic, and fundamental security is adhered to, it will continue to be a subjective situation and

DOI: 10.1201/9781003204145-1

breaches will continue unabated as we witness on a near daily basis in the press or on the news.

Steve Jobs launched Apple on 1 April 1976 and managed to disrupt the market almost immediately and pretty much ever since with their innovation, designs, and functionality. After a period, they also managed to get pretty good with security too; however, the agencies had different ideas. One cannot underestimate how revolutionary the 'Two Steve's' were and how they shaped the PC and mobile market back then.

A year later, brilliant cryptographers Whitfield Diffie and Martin Hellman published a paper on the method of exchanging cryptographic digital keys. A year later, Ron Rivest, Adi Shamir, and Leonard Adleman published the first asymmetric algorithm and called it RSA (Rivest-Shamir-Aldeman) which went on to become the gold standard and widely adopted today as is Diffie Hellman. To explain digital certificates and encryption keys, it is easy to think of digital certificates as digital passports providing authentication of both the users and devices and something of an evolution of the Enigma and Lorenz machines used in World War II. The Enigma and Lorenz machines enabled encryption and decryption of messages by using ciphers and authentication and ultimately, the breaking of both machines was later confirmed as saving tens of thousands of lives.

At the same time, the US and the UK Agencies were working on developing Public Key Infrastructure (PKI) to facilitate secure electronic transfer of information. Now, they have the technology; however, they need to ensure that it is secure to ensure authentication of each device and each user with the aim to ensure each party were whom they said they were and to ensure privacy. Of course, such security and privacy relied upon uninterrupted connection. In simple terms, cryptography and PKI binds public keys with respective identities (known to a group such as a GCHQ or NSA). The binding is established by registration and digital certificates that are provided by a Certificate Authority (CA). The level of assurance can be automated with minimum levels, such as a SHA-1 certificate, when in 2011 they were deprecated due to being able to be broken by force and so on. However, unlike the Enigma and Lorenz machines, that when they were deciphered (cracked) by the brilliant Alan Turing (Enigma) and William Tutte (Lorenz), they were decrypted period. Modern PCs

THE WORLDWIDE EXPLOSION OF PERSONAL COMPUTERS 3

and digital machines could simply swap out and upgrade their ciphers and digital certificates and remain secure.

Cryptography and cryptographers for decades was a closed shop of agency's mathematicians such as Clifford Cocks and James Ellis of GCHQ. Put simply, the agencies had designed PKI from the ground up originally for their own use and did not see the need for the public to understand or comprehend it, and for the vast majority, it was more akin to rocket science in any event, so very few bothered even trying. Due to the continued growth in the personal computers and laptops and digital devices, it was decided in the 1990s PKI was deemed the most suitable protocol to provide security and shared as a Gold Standard for global adoption. It is not clear at which stage the agencies decided to manipulate the digital certificates to enable digital eavesdropping (see Network Exploitation), however remember the agencies enjoyed up to two decades of PKI development before it was used publicly.

Certificate authorities (CAs) were selected and can be considered as part of the internet's infrastructure. CAs were given privileged status as they effectively held the keys (no pun intended) to corporations, governments, and people's security and privacy. There is a debate on who issued the first certificates, RSA or Netscape, however both issued certificates in the mid-1990s to work with the newly available PKI and to support the ongoing digital revolution. C As sprung up everywhere and digital certificates were issued initially in their millions, tens of millions, and into their billions. Unfortunately, and even though most CAs would flourish, controls and management were lacking (a common theme throughout technology and security) and so many basic mistakes were made with massive implications. The concept was good; however, the management was far from ideal. To this day, CAs make so many mistakes by issuing incorrect certificates, having to find and revoke others that have been found to be used for nefarious purposes or stolen. Certificates can be used for many things and shared across many devices. CAs issued incorrect certificates to the wrong parties and revoking them became a major challenge. As an example, in early 2020, Lets Encrypt issued 3 million certificates incorrectly and had to revoke them, all of them. Digicert was breached in 2020 and both organisations are still unsure of what certificates were compromised, issued, and need revoking let alone where they were all issued. Over the last 25 years, CAs have a questionable track record for being breached themselves, and of course, they are a perfect target for cybercriminals who want access to thousands of clients. They can go undetected as Stuxnet and Sunburst can testify. Certificates in their millions, even billions, provide the security and validity for millions of companies, and billions of websites, often without validity and incorrectly issued. Unfortunately, just like our mobiles and laptops today, a false sense of trust can be created by CAs and assumptions incorrectly made. It can quickly become a single point of failure for most companies, in fact I would go so far as to say, every company and government, have little to no idea of what their PKI estate actually looks like or contains. Digital certificates from various CAs are frequently available on the Dark Web and to give some idea to the reader, a handgun can be bought on the same Dark Web for a few hundred US dollars, a digital certificate, depending on the CA issuer, and class, is usually two to three thousand dollars. A digital certificate with privileges, such as those used in SolarWinds, can cause billion dollar losses and damage. It is imperative that PKI is properly controlled and managed, without it, all other security can be, and is, undermined.

Corporations, governments, every company, and every person have become totally reliant upon PKI and digital certificates for security, often unknowingly, immaterial if they chose to or not. PKI was designed to be the very bedrock of privacy and security and create Digital Trust. This is a term we will hear a lot more throughout the book. Digital Trust was the Shangri-la for all users as their mobile, PC, and later, their laptop would be things they would trust, they could share and document their most intimate feelings, photographs, experiences, and data with and send on. However, others had different ideas and by manipulating the very same PKI that was there to provide security and privacy, they developed and manipulated it to invade, exfiltrate, and undermine both. This situation was actively encouraged by the explosion of social media and mass data collection, more recently and commonly now known as cookies which frequently overstep the mark of data collection unknowingly and are often cited in legal disputes on privacy and GDPR.

Let us briefly consider the difference between a standard digital certificate and a root certificate. The root certificate is often known as

THE WORLDWIDE EXPLOSION OF PERSONAL COMPUTERS 5

the trusted root and sits at the centre of the entire trust model underpinning the entire PKI. This then extends out to TLS and SSL certificates. Every device you buy today comes complete with a Root Store collection of preloaded certificates and their public encryption keys. This enables software and apps, for example to authenticate the device and you, as the new owner. These root stores run under very strict guidelines from major vendors and OEMs such as Mozilla, Google, and Microsoft. Of course, from time to time, these can, like a regular certificate, be compromised by becoming invalid, for example in the same way as a regular certificate. It may require revoking and replacing. A root certificate is invaluable because any subsequent certificate signed using the root's private key will be trusted. This has been the holy grail for a cybercriminal to ascertain so they in effect can act like the owner and sign certificates at will. You can see how a misconfigured or illegally gained root certificate might be of interest for anyone with nefarious intent. It is often said in the industry that unlike the Turing and Tutte, one does not need to decrypt, one simply needs to find the encrypted keys which provide that elusive Digital Trust and enables plain text to be read, copied, shared, and so on. The job of a cybercriminal has been made substantially easier, not harder, due to the lack of PKI controls and management let alone the woefully inadequate internet facing security which is flagged as a Not Secure in the address bar...

Staying on that theme for just a moment, and to elaborate upon what a valid certificate on an internet facing domain provides: It provides Authentication of the domain's certificate owner and the website and means, the removal of a Man in the Middle attack, it also ensures all data is encrypted. This is a critical distinction, and that the data has integrity, in other words, you have Digital Trust. If however, a certificate is invalid, you have none of these. You may be on a Shadow site as was used in the recent BA breach which had some 400,000 people buying and paying for flights to cybercriminals and not BA. I will go into more detail later; however, this single distinction and critical issue is a major factor as to why cyberattacks, both in terms of frequency and scale, have escalated from a few million dollars in the 1990s to an estimated $6 trillion by the end of 2021. Cybercriminals are targeting insecure domains with invalid certificates continuously in their attempt to find opportunities to hijack the domain, gain command and control (C2) and then, ultimately gain enterprise access. If this sounds familiar it should do as this is exactly what happened at last month's (December 2020) disclosure of the breach at SolarWinds that is believed to have commenced in March 2020. By identifying insecure SolarWinds domains (and there were over a dozen to choose from as our report confirms) the adversary hijacked a domain, stood up to their own domain www.avsvmcloud.com which has subsequently been re-seized, and gained full enterprise access and privileges. Once this was achieved, they were able to laterally move and use SolarWinds digital certificates, lace them with Malware (Stuxnet style), and have them distributed to unsuspecting clients. The clients often had automated downloads from SolarWinds due to the existing Digital Trust (assumptions) and the updates, as normal, only to then be breached. Digital certificates and PKI form the very foundation of security and is overlooked and ignored at one's peril. The agencies actively discouraged and dissuaded companies and governments of the importance of certificates, PKI, and internet facing security at massive costs and as such, they are frequently overlooked, ignored, and neglected. Whilst companies are busy chasing so-called sophisticated attacks, no one is controlling or managing their certificates or PKI, the foundation of all their security. Lessons to be learned and lessons continually being ignored...

2

9/11 AND THE CREATION OF MASS DATA COLLECTION IN THE NAME OF SECURITY...

There are certain events in one's life that you will never forget. Where you were when Lennon was shot or when Martin Luther king spoke on Capitol Hill or the day Mandela was released. The event that will always stay with me was the afternoon of 11 September 2001.

I had just finished playing an enjoyable game of golf in a vendor tournament. The sun was warm on this beautiful afternoon and the setting was stunning on the East Sussex Golf Course. I walked in from the 18th green to order and enjoy a drink with my colleagues before the after-dinner event. Upon entering the Club House, I was confronted by a huge TV screen showing, what clearly appeared to be Steven Spielberg movie. There on the screen were two towers that looked like the movie Towering Inferno. I then realised it was live and the towers were in fact the World Trade Towers in New York. I recognised them as I had visited them twice previously and knew them and their location. Strangely I could not help my mid second guessing and calculating how many people might be inside. I felt sick to my stomach and could not stop watching in total disbelief. Many months later and upon reflection, I can understand why so many in the US intelligence felt so exposed, and that the day was among the very worst in the US Intelligence history. The date was 11 September 2001, a bright Tuesday morning in New York.

Four passenger airliners had departed from north-eastern US airports bound for California and were individually hijacked by a total of 19 al-Qaeda terrorists. Two of the planes, American Airlines flights Nos. 11 and 175, crashed mercilessly into the North and South towers of the World Trade Centres in Lower Manhattan. The first impact left a gaping hole around the 80th floor instantly killing hundreds

DOI: 10.1201/9781003204145-2

of people both inside the building and passengers on the plane itself. It left those above on higher floors up to the 110th totally stranded and cut off without any way, or indeed hope of finding a way to safety. As evacuations of the tower on lower floors commenced, it was initially considered to be a one-off freak accident. Hundreds of emergency workers were running towards the scene of the accident as it was deemed at the time. Just 18 minutes after the first crash, a second live broadcast showed a second plane, flight No. 175, appear and seemingly turning sharply towards the South Tower. It hit the tower around the 60th floor again instantly killing hundreds of people and trapping hundreds more people above. In under an hour and 42 minutes, both 110 storey towers totally collapsed killing nearly 3,000 people and injuring over 25,000. 343 firefighters and 72 law enforcement officers were killed. No one can ever remove the images or footage we witnessed that day. We were totally powerless to do anything about it. Hindsight is a wonderful thing and if it had been known as a terrorist attack, those in the South Tower and those running up to help others in the North Tower, different decisions may have been made.

The third plane, flight No. 77, crashed into the Pentagon leading to the collapse of the building on the west side, and the fourth plane, flight No. 93, was originally headed for Washington DC but crashed into a field in Stonycreek Pennsylvania after passengers thwarted the hijackers. It is virtually impossible to know how one might react in such situations, self-preservation, outrage, or anger and striking out. The fact is, sadly, three of the Terrorists' missions succeeded in the eyes of al-Qaeda by causing massive damage and fatalities at the very heart of the US and only one was not. The US acted quickly and announced a 'War on Terror.' They started by invading Afghanistan to depose the Taliban and hunt down Osama Bin Laden among many other activities including cyberwarfare. Meetings in the Situation Room were obviously vocal and fraught at the time, what action could be taken and how could one achieve justice, possibly often masked as revenge.

As mentioned earlier in the previous chapter, security always plays catch up and this awful event was no exception. Airports became awash with scanning machines as a prerequisite including people. Possibly more importantly and more secretly, President George W Bush called his teams of senior intelligence groups from the NSA, CIA, FBI, and others together to agree how they could utilise and

9/11 AND THE CREATION OF MASS DATA COLLECTION   9

manipulate, Computer Network Exploitation (CNE). The objective was to attempt to capitalise and digitally eavesdrop on digital communications to and from the US to and from known countries and suspected terrorists that they believed harboured further terrorist cells and organisations. The first program was simply titled The Terrorist Surveillance Program (TSP) and was headed by the NSA. TSP would go on to enable the secret digital eavesdropping and tracking of billions of calls and emails made by, and received by, millions of US citizens over the coming decades. TSP would go on to become a blueprint of what would follow. However originally it was part of the President's Surveillance Program which in turn came under the overall umbrella of War on Terrorism. The TSP was initially designed and sanctioned that at least one party in the communication was not a US citizen and that may have the original agreement and parameters; however, this was quickly changed and more than likely, abused.

As digital communications became more widespread, the newly found method of gathering data en masse became too easy and Network Exploitation became global. That was for every country and potentially, every person. If you used a laptop, a phone, or a personal computer, chances are that your actions and your calls could be monitored, and the data gathered for further and future analysis. Big Brother was very much alive and barely anybody knew at that stage and even if they suspected, it would be impossible at that time to realise to what extent. I will not go into detail here of the warrantless surveillance controversies that followed. Many such programs operated without judicial oversight, none the less, such programs existed following the 9/11 attacks and in the main, for what seemed to be justified. It has repeatedly been said that 9/11 caught the Intelligence agencies napping, it would not happen again, could it? A great source of further specific information can be found in the excellent book, *The Shadow Factory* written by James Bamford.

On 6 June 2007, TSP was renamed and became known as PRISM. PRISM was now under judicial guidelines and rules or so it was stated. It was supposed to only gather intelligence if one party was not a US-based citizen. Much controversy has been witnessed and claims made that this was not strictly adhered to. President Bush had to review the program every 45 days and the intelligence committees, House of Representatives, and Senate were briefed on numerous occasions. No note taking was allowed or external confirmation that the program even existed; however, it most certainly did as was revealed by Edward Snowden, and it was far reaching. The agencies had new capabilities and they were certainly not afraid to use them, even if, and when, that meant bending the rules. The adage of do not bother asking for permission, ask for forgiveness if you get caught, and cite plausible deniability was very much in play, many were contractors for that reason. What the NSA realised, along with some of their counterparts, was people were becoming so used to digital communications, to share their most intimate secrets, their business plans, their bank details, contacts, and so on. This data would of course be of extreme use and benefit for them as metadata, but also as a method for the rapidly expanding social media companies. Elections, influencing trends, and so on could be used to persuade the populace as desired. The power of data was certainly not wasted on their efforts.

Earlier on 4 February 2004, Mark Zuckerberg started Facebook and one of the early investors was Peter Thiel who invested $500k for a 10.2% stake valuing the company at $4.9 billion. It was also a poorly kept secret that the CIA was also an originator and early investor into Facebook. The agencies knew that digital communications and the encryption of the data, and the ability to decrypt with the right keys would provide invaluable and unrivalled access. The world continued to shift from analogue to digital, and they wanted to capture it, all of it...

This should come as no surprise. The CIA now had quite a history of developing and manipulating encryption along with GCHQ. One of the industry's worst kept secrets was the fact the CIA owned Crypto AG the Swiss company that developed and built government encryption and cipher machines. The CIA had secretly bought Crypto AG in 1970 and with its 120 government clients it was a shrewd, if not somewhat underhand move due to the fact the CIA had backdoors built into the machines which enabled decryption. If this sounds familiar to recent spats with the social media and mobile operators, it should also not come as a surprise. This also included backdoors to their Allies information. One could think of such actions as ruthless and undermining any relationship with any organisations, let alone one's Allies. The code name for this program was Thesaurus and then Rubicon. It went on for several decades until 11 February 2020 when finally, *The Washington Post* confirmed the CIA's ownership. The Swiss government was extremely embarrassed by the revelations and the event certainly questioned their neutrality. On 25 November 2020, the Swiss company and competitor to Crypto AG, OMNISEC, was also confirmed as being owned by the CIA and the NSA who had been building and selling manipulated (backdoor) equipment to foreign governments and armies, even the Swiss government themselves. This may not be news to some; however, this revelation confirmed the lengths the US agencies were prepared to go to ensuring data capture across the globe. For NAs, as far as the US was concerned, no one was exempt.

Mass intelligence gathering became the mainstay focus of nearly all the government agencies and their thousands of staff. It was deemed to provide them with the upper hand, intelligence, and data which to them, equalled power. They could capture the data, all the data, knew how to encrypt it, and have it decrypted. That included governments and the data of the governments of their Allies. Never had such comprehensive and complete digital eavesdropping been possible. The days of MI5 putting a small bug in a picture or a radio transmitter in the door hinge pin were long gone (great story). Now total digital access was virtually complete and the original auspices of defending the country had been stretched as far as they dare at that point and the advantage was plain to realise. However, so long as the secrets were theirs, and theirs alone, everyone should be safe.

It is a known fact that in the digital and espionage world, what can be used for defensive purposes can also be used for offensive purposes. That thought process had already begun. If the agencies could manipulate digital communications, turning on a camera on a personal computer or laptop from thousands of miles away, could they not use their new-found capabilities for offensive purposes too? Could such a capability support or even supersede the need for armed, sea, and air-led warfare along with unquestionable cost saving to lives let alone taxpayers $...

3

PRISM, Project Aurora, and Early Digital Offensive Capability

PRISM was now in full swing capturing metadata in bucket loads and being further developed by the US agencies and then a new iteration came in the name and form of XKEYSCORE. This highly secretive computer system collected data internationally and continually. The NSA shared portions of XKEYSCORE with other intelligence agencies (Five Eyes) including the Australian Signals Directorate, Canada's Community Security Establishment, New Zealand's Government Security Bureau, and Britain's Government Communications Headquarters (GCHQ). It was also shared with Japan's Defence Intelligence Headquarters and Germany's Bundesnachrichtendienst. These secret systems were unknown outside these agencies and governments and it was not until Edward Snowden publicly revealed the NSA's programs in July 2013, that they even broke cover and the true magnitude, capability, and purpose started to become understood. It was revealed that XKEYSCORE had the ability to enable unlimited surveillance on almost any human being anywhere in the world. Of course, the NSA played this down, and declared Snowden had acted with treason. The ranks were closed. Various and numerous legal and judicial events took place; however, XKEYSCORE continues (albeit under a new code name) in one form or another to this day and the agencies employ tens of thousands of people. These programmes are usually contractors from the various governments, previously 'selected providers,' which apart from greatly increasing the costs, enables a certain degree of comfort and plausible deniability. A few years ago, *The Washington Post* confirmed that there were 1,271 government organisations and 1,931 private companies in 10,000 locations across the US that worked on counterterrorism, homeland security, and intelligence. The Intelligence community

DOI: 10.1201/9781003204145-3

13

employed, directly and indirectly via the private sector, 854,000 people and all holding top secret clearance, which would be kept at the Office of Personnel Management, would also go on to be breached. That number has most certainly increased since Wikipedia suggests that 29% of that workforce are currently contractors and account for 49% of the total budget. In other words, just a tad over a quarter of the workforce costs nearly a half of the total budget.

Cyber intelligence is unquestionably comprehensive; however, let's now consider more on cyber offensive capability of boys and their toys. This area posed more and more attraction to the US government and projects were discussed on how, by manipulating code, and gaining Digital Trust, the agency could cause collateral damage without even being present and to all intent and purposes, anonymously. Cyberattacks were not, and are still not easily classified into cyber vandalism, cyber nuisance, cyberterrorism, or cyberwar. There is no Cyber Geneva Convention even though one is urgently required. The lines are currently very grey and unclear, and this is a major error and needs clarity urgently. But until that point, cyberattacks will continue and remain unclassified, as will the many, often unknown retaliations.

The first trial of such offensive capability came in the shape of a 25-tonne diesel generator used for generating electrical power. It was like hundreds of such generators used across the US. The project was run under the banner of 'exploring defensive capability' should the US be subject to a cyberattack themselves. The project was named Aurora and in 2007 at the Idaho laboratory, the generator, using commands from computer code and circuit breakers, was manipulated to demonstrate how a cyberattack could destroy physical components that made up the grid. An interesting video is available online. The computer program that controlled the circuit breakers was tampered with to rapidly open and close the breakers out of sequence, ultimately disrupting the harmonics. In essence, the generator was sped up and slowed down rapidly causing harmonic, stress, and shock waves which caused the internal components to explode. Think of doing 55 mph in your car and selecting reverse gear and letting the clutch out and this was in essence what happened to the generator. Lessons learnt from the Aurora project would be learned and tweaked to perfect later attacks. The world's most famous attack that would be acknowledged as the world's first digital weapon was code-named Olympic Games and go on to be known as Stuxnet taking letters from the actual code. Stuxnet was used in the attack on the Iranian Nuclear Power facility in Natanz.

Project Aurora had demonstrated huge vulnerabilities and was a major concern as most of the US electric grid relied upon such equipment and protocols, and most of the grid's equipment was never designed with little or no security features. Much of it was also made in more cost-effective countries, such as China. This meant that any would-be attacker simply had to be able to communicate with a computer to gain access and override it. The generator used in Project Aurora was destroyed in less than three minutes with parts exploding and falling some 80 feet away. The destruction through this simulated cyberattack could have been much quicker; however, the researchers wanted to test and video record each wave of code manipulation. Destruction could have been achieved in a fraction of that time, within seconds. However, as with all thing's security, it was considered a great success for offensive capability. More a case of flexing muscles to dissuade attacks as opposed to ensuring security. Sadly, a common theme even from the Nuclear age.

The failures of multiple, often connected generators would lead to blackouts and widespread disruption across much of the US. A single generator alone could cause severe disruption and only a few years beforehand actually did when in 2003 the Northeast blackout occurred. With extended lead times and substantial replacement costs, let alone the inconvenience, not controlling, or securing elements of any, and all the entire National Grid as part of the Critical National Infrastructure (CNI) was seen to be critically important and yet to this day, still has totally inadequate security. It is as if everyone has gone back in time, and not made any security advancements. It is as if time stood still, but why? The risks to the entire US have been acknowledged and are severe and yet being overlooked.

Joe Weiss, a colleague, friend, and industry expert on Industrial Control Systems (ICS) was outspoken and enraged disputing the findings from the report on Project Aurora Mitigation, saying it misled utilities and would cause a great deal of oversight by not addressing the threats sufficiently. Joe and I have discussed this on several occasions and concur that a major blackout such as 'Lights

Out' mentioned recently by Xcel Energy is a strong possibility, even definite.

What the Project Aurora Mitigation report overlooked and indeed possibly did not consider, was the fact that many of the computers connected to the National Grid were highly vulnerable to exploitation themselves as they had next to no security controls or management. Once one computer was infiltrated, it was a simple case of infecting and potentially taking over command and control (C2) of the entire enterprise. The consequences of such an event are beyond imagination. The entire grid could be shut down, as it would be later in the Ukraine. Everything that is relied upon today could be shut down and affect everyone. And yet even last night (28/12/2020), following an announcement by a leading domestic and international provider of energy, our research showed that they had numerous vulnerabilities facing the internet with invalid, expired certificates and Common Vulnerabilities and Exposures (CVEs) are in abundance. This means they are wide open and highly vulnerable to a cyberattack, a man in the middle attack, or a domain hijacking as also happened at SolarWinds in December 2020. In fact, this week I have written to the Commissioner of Nuclear Power as they themselves are maintaining a suboptimal homepage meaning they are totally open to being breached. They have taken it so seriously that they have ignored it for over three months and still no reply.

If 2020 has taught us anything over and beyond Covid-19 humanity and consideration, it is the fact the vast majority of users, executives, government officials, even agency operatives and cybersecurity professionals, overlook, ignore, or do not consider internet facing and connected security as a concern and are all but totally unaware of the vulnerabilities and implications of PKI. Please put the coffee on…

I always pose this question. If you lived in a high crime area, and all the houses in your neighbourhood had been broken into and burgled, and you chose to leave, for a year or two and left all the windows and doors blatantly open with all your possessions on show, would you, upon your return expect nothing to have happened? Of course, you would not. Yet this is the exact situation created and ignored by corporations, governments, and even agencies that leave their digital doors wide open day after day, week after week, and month after month. Our research has uncovered domains of major organisations including missile manufacturers, the ex-President of the US, and the White House that are insecure and have been for years. The chances of these organisations and firms already being infiltrated are incredibly high and must question leadership and the entire security adopted by the management of third-party supply chains including those to the DOD and DHS. This subject could cover a whole chapter alone as well as naming and shaming. Possibly even a book on its own, however on this occasion, it is only a missile manufacturer, the ex-President, and White House, so what could possibly go wrong?

In 2017, the world was floundering under increasing cyberattacks, and although modest in comparison to today's almost daily attacks, it was decided as part of a wider security initiative, to move from HTTP to HTTPS. The S stands for Security. Mozilla, Google, and many others started to alert all those using the internet with either a Padlock or a Not Secure script on the top left of the domain text in the address bar, you will have seen it many times. However, you may not have noticed it. A Not Secure text means the site cannot be authenticated, is not encrypted, and may have data integrity issues, in other words, all data and text could be read in plain text form. It could be a Shadow site, a spoof, a hijacked site that could assist man in the middle attacks or denial of service. The warning of it being Not Secure does not always register as has been proven in hundreds of cases of breaches and the maintenance of insecure, uncontrolled, and unmanaged domains. Even companies that have been breached, paid Ransomware and yet still ignore security on their homepage by remaining, Not Secure by default, waiting for the next attack. Some of the very worst are www.vatican.va, www.archer.ac.uk, and www.uhnj.org. Organisations wanting maximum internet presence will typically have dozens, sometime hundreds of domains, to capture more and more footfall and business. NASA, for example, have 23,699 registered domains. Some 20,000 or so are dormant, and 3,699 are live. The ability to manage and control all of these is a major, near impossible task. The maximising of internet presence whilst ignoring security has created a Shangri-la for cybercriminals. Companies have an unquestionable moral and legal responsibility to protect their client's information, if they cannot, they don't deserve it. All you need to know is that of the 2 billion or so websites today, a very high percentage are not authentic. They are trying to lure and tempt their visitors under a false pretence and a Not Secure website is a major telltale sign. Having said that, Maze, the infamous Ransomware group, was using Cloudflare to provide hosting for their illegal activities online and using a digital certificate provided by a DNS partner of Cloudflare making their site look legitimate. Cloudflare also provide hosting services for the FBI…

To put this into some context, around 30,000 websites are digitally prised daily with the equivalent of a digital crowbar to identify and find vulnerabilities that can be exploited and used to infiltrate to gain access. There is no prize for guessing which domains are infiltrated and access gained. Those that are insecure and by being so are making themselves easy targets. Domain hijacking is a known threat actor and exactly the method used in the initial infiltration of SolarWinds (covered later). To date, our research on every company breached in 2020 (we started research in January) shows that every company breached had major numerous vulnerabilities and suboptimal internet facing, and connected security making a direct correlation between breached companies and their internet insecure position. It is clearly not a coincidence, and think of it this way, just as the US could spy on people thousands of miles away, what does a cybercriminal based in say Asia or somewhere similar, thousands of miles away, do to find an organisation's vulnerability? That is correct, they will poke around at your websites and using Open-Source Intelligence (OSINT) tools, they can even receive AI alerts as to subdomain structures and when they become invalid in preparation to launch their attacks, this is their business model.

In a nutshell, whether internet security and PKI are controlled and managed by your company or not, if you maintain Not Secure domains, the chances of being breached are increased exponentially, and if they are not currently, they may well soon be, it is all but a fait accompli…

4
STUXNET TO ZERO DAYS

During the early days of design and development on Project Aurora, the design of Olympic Games was already being conceptualised and then designed. It used the same principal of digital code being used to cause collateral damage and explosions. Just four short years had passed since the 9/11 terrorist attacks and the cold-blooded murder of thousands of innocent civilians. The wounds ran deep and united the US in its quest for justice against terrorists and the 'Axis of Evil.' Osama Bin Laden was still goading the US and would not be captured until much later on 1 May 2011. The US had anger running through its veins and wanted to inflict as much pain on their adversaries, and believed they knew, unequivocally who they were.

Congress signed off on ever increasing budgets in their $billions, often not knowing exactly what for, and not always really wanting to ask. It is fair to say retaliation and dominance in the cyberspace, both defensive and even more so, offensive was the focus and US's quest, no matter what it would take or cost. A massive recruitment drive at the agencies and the supplying partners with unimaginable amounts of cash being thrown around during 2005 and 2006 for bright young computer experts was just one part of their initiative. The contractor market was the most buoyant by far and offered what amounted to around twice, often more, than that of an equivalent skilled employee. One notable technical recruited individual was a certain Edward Snowden, who was taken on in May 2006. Initially Edward Snowden joined the CIA in the global communications team that required high-level security clearance (more on the OPM breach in 2014 and the breach of 22 million security cleared operatives in a later chapter). Snowden was instrumental in the continued transition to the often misunderstood and more complex digital cyber intelligence and its perfecting. The US government decided to announce and declare plausible deniability, which would make sense to use contractors.

DOI: 10.1201/9781003204145-4

19

This in effect created monopolies among several of the preferred companies and providers of resources. Many of these companies were often headed by ex-senior agency members. It also meant that the actual cost of resources was around twice that than it would or should be to have that slight distinction of direct or indirect resource. It was a computer technician's dream to be a contractor as the pay was unrivalled even though they in effect worked and answered directly to the NSA or CIA. In fact, most contractors never met anyone from the company that was paying them directly or went to their offices. It simply meant that the government's liabilities both in terms of legal and pensions were different.

There was substantial tension between the US and their Allies Israel, and considerably more so between Israel's arch adversary Iran. Israel's Prime Minister, Benjamin Netanyahu was convinced that Iran wanted to build nuclear warheads and use them to bomb Israel, so much so that he wanted to initiate bombing Tehran first. During this same period, President Bush and his team supposedly met Netanyahu's Unit 8200, the Israeli Intelligence Corps, whereupon discussions and debriefing on Project Aurora and Olympic Games were held. The design and overview of Olympic Games was clearly of interest as directly bombing would unquestionably be an act of war, whereas this could be avoided should it be an anonymous cyberattack. A joint effort was agreed upon.

It was a known fact that Iran had commenced developing Nuclear Power sites in August 2002. Prior to this date, the development had been more secretive and clandestine. The plants would provide Nuclear Power by enriching uranium. One facility was at Natanz and the other at Arak. The Natanz facility was of extreme interest to the US and Israel, and the concern was that by enriching uranium to provide Nuclear Power, it would prove to be a huge stepping stone for enabling uranium enrichment to the next level for Nuclear bomb capability. In 2003, the International Atomic Energy Agency (IAEA) launched an investigation after an Iranian dissident group revealed undeclared nuclear activities being carried out. In 2006 it was judged that Iran had not complied with their obligations and the United Nations Security Council demanded that Iran suspend their enrichment programmes. The US National Intelligence Estimate (NIE) stated that Iran had also halted an alleged nuclear weapon programme in late 2003.

Uranium is the fuel used for nuclear reactors. It can be found and mined at many places around the world. To make the actual fuel, uranium is mined and goes through refining and enrichment before being loaded into a nuclear reactor. Part of the enrichment programme is called conversion. It is where uranium oxide is converted to a different compound (uranium hexafluoride) which is a gas at relatively low temperatures. The uranium hexafluoride is fed into centrifuges with thousands of rapidly spinning vertical tubes that separate uranium-235 from the slightly heavier uranium-238 isotope. The centrifuges separate the two streams, the first is enriched with uranium-235, and the other consists of tails containing a lower concentration of uranium-235 and is known as depleted uranium.

Olympic Games was designed from the outset to target the centrifuges and by manipulating the oscillation (speed) via the Programmable Logic Controller (PLC) which managed the speed of the vertical tubes. By altering the speeds, just like Project Aurora, it would cause harmonic and physical damage, ultimately causing an explosion. This was a near carbon copy of the diesel generator in Project Aurora which had been proved so successful. In a secret US location, centrifuges were installed as per the Iranian nuclear facility which had been replicated from photographs kindly provided by Iranian television. Previous intelligence and the use of previously confiscated centrifuges from a previous haul of a well-known dictator and adversary of the US made the task quite easy. To cut to the chase and to simplify the overall time, trials, and processes of the programme, once a single centrifuge destruction was achieved by using the optimum speed and code change, the remnants of the destructed centrifuge was delivered to President Bush's office at the White House. President Bush immediately approved, and signed of the programme, Olympic Games was on.

The team now had achieved the outcome and result they desired, the explosion of as many of the centrifuges used to enrich the uranium, and therefore delay the Iranian Nuclear Programme. All they had to figure out was how to get the malicious code into the system and onto the PLCs that controlled and managed the speeds. Between the NSA and the Israeli 8220 cyber force, they had created an incredible code that would go on to be known as Stuxnet, being a mix of letters of the code. Stuxnet had a delay capability of 13 days to let everything

22   STUXNET TO SUNBURST

run as normal for 13 days before triggering the new code. It would also replay the first 13 normal days to the operators who in turn would see everything running as normal and not consider or suspect foul play. Stuxnet also utilised the holy grail of all cyberattack code, Zero Days. Such a worm or code is a code that has never been encountered before and has no known defence or way to deal with it. In effect, no one has any experience or any (Zero) Days dealing with it, it is brand new. Stuxnet used no less than four separate Zero Days making it the single most complex code written or deployed at the time and wreaked of State Nation's capability, resource, and investment.

So now the teams had the outcome and the complex Stuxnet code complete with four Zero Days and 13 days delay (strangely the same as SolarWinds's breach). Natanz computers were Air Gapped, meaning they did not connect with the internet or any outside systems, so the lessons learned and used from previous Network Exploitation would not work. At first, they even tried using a USB stick laced with the Stuxnet code. That trick had previously been used against the US Intelligence agencies who had foolishly fallen for years before when USB sticks had been dropped in car parks at various facilities and then plugged in to see what was on them. The US agencies tried to encourage external resources to insert the malware laced stick in Natanz. This was far too risky and so, for the first time in history, the lessons that had been previously learned from manipulating digital certificates and encrypted keys that made up their own developed PKI was seen to be a unique and totally safe way to inject the malicious code into the systems without being recognised, questioned, or halted. This heralded a new method of hiding cyberattacks and malicious code in full view. More on this monumental use of digital certificates is discussed later.

It was decided to use illegally gained Microsoft digital certificates for many reasons. Firstly, they would not be directly tied to the attackers, secondly everyone used Microsoft and even though the enterprise at Natanz was Air Gapped, all the devices internally still used and relied upon digital certificates to authenticate and encrypt software to and from device to device. So, when certificates were required, the two Microsoft certificates, already laced with Stuxnet, were provided and unknowingly used. The issuer knew no difference from a regular Microsoft digital certificate and the user simply downloaded them (see SOLARWINDS breach copied the Stuxnet attack, covered in a later chapter).

After running for 13 days, the malicious code was triggered and went hunting for their targets and in particular, Siemens Step 7 PLCs, and once found launched the Zero Days attacks which in turn would create the oscillating issues. The vertical tubes were sped up and slowed down as designed, causing the breaking of the vertical tubes at speed within the centrifuges causing explosions and uranium leakage. Forensically, the engineers of course were checking their desktops and all readings were perfectly normal due to the replaying of the original 13 day's data and yet massive explosions and collateral damage was being experienced. The Iranian executives started blaming their scientists and general chaos and disarray including, and rather shockingly, murder was the result.

On 29 November 2010, the Iranian President, Mahmoud Ahmadinejad stated that the computers at Natanz had problems with handling the centrifuges and that a small number of centrifuges had been affected. On the same day two Iranian Nuclear Scientists were targeted in two separate car bombings. Majid Shahriari, a quantum physicist, was killed and Fereydoon Abbasi, a high-ranking official from the MOD, was seriously wounded. The Iranian Nuclear Power was at best, derailed and delayed only for several months. Iran's capability and operation would increase, it certainly was not halted. More of a bloody nose than a knockout and a rather expensive one as it would ultimately prove.

Neither the US nor Israel confirmed their involvement, although globally, some ten years on, it is universally accepted that Olympic Games was their joint cyber forces' work and fathered by further attributed cyberattacks and malware including Duqu and Flame. Flame is often considered the original variant. The overall success of the mission Olympic Games is questionable, although by creating the world's first Digital Weapon it had certainly created an awareness and capability that had possibly not, to date, been considered, and that was the use of digital certificates being used for nefarious purposes, we would see this more later. Given the fact that pretty much only the government agencies at the time knew what PKI stood for, let alone what it did and how it could be manipulated. At the time, General Michael Hayden, the Director of US Intelligence said: 'There are those out there that will look at this and maybe even attempt to turn it to their own purposes. Pandora's box was now open, and no one would be able close it.'

This outcome could not have been much worse for the entire world as not only did the agencies deny involvement, but they also dissuaded corporations and governments of the importance of digital certificates and PKI in general. This enabled their continued clandestine digital manipulation and eavesdropping which shockingly, is still done to this day. Do not forget, it would still be a decade before Crypto AG and Omnisec, the two Swiss cryptography companies, would be confirmed as being owned by the CIA and their services and encryption being sold to governments all around the world with CIA backdoors. The masquerade continued with projects designed and controlled by the NSA and GCHQ such as QUANTUM INSERT, HEARTBEAT, HUSH PUPPIES, and FLYING PIGS.

The world's first digital weapon used digital certificates to manipulate, lace, and hide the Stuxnet malicious code and new agency programmes were developed to manipulate the entire spectrum of Transport Layer Security (TLS) and Secure Sockets Layer (SSL) certificates. Such programmes would continue to be implanted gaining unrestricted access and by also utilising Domain Name System (DNS) and Content Delivery Network (CDN), they had all bases covered moving forward at their disposal.

Unfortunately the massive oversight and faux pas that it seems all agencies forgot to consider is that old adage, what can be used for defensive, can also be reversed and used for offensive, and in terms of global security, the gaping holes being left by the near total lack of domain, internet connectivity, and PKI controls and management, the very areas the agencies were exploiting and manipulating were also now being used by the rapidly increasing number of cybercriminals and gangs springing up. Cybercriminals only required a single domain, an invalid or expired certificate, an uncontrolled, long forgotten subdomain (SOLARWINDS) and they could gain access and infiltrate. The opportunity to take over command and control (C2) is a no longer a pipe dream, it is a very strong possibility and is occurring right now in many companies that are not only household names, but major organisations and governments.

Ultimately the agencies' and the President's previous actions could be considered reckless and have, inadvertently and unequivocally, created the massive increase of cyberattacks over the last decade, including the continued increases in frequency and scale. Cybercriminals have learned and been 'educated' by our own agencies, their actions and the security fraternity have been left to try and secure the world wearing blinkers and being handcuffed. When I started in the industry, I thought, bring it on, I know what is wrong and what is right, and I am unwavering in my quest. What I did not realise is that not only were we going to have to fight the bad guys, the criminals, but also the so-called good guys who would dissuade corporations, Critical National Infrastructure organisations, Big 4, and Tier one banks because they themselves were tapping and infiltrating the very same organisations themselves using the very TLS and SSL certificates that we would uncover. This book is an attempt to ensure the agencies' clandestine manipulation, and the cyberwar the agencies started, as it sits, can be addressed and a level playing field created. Left as is, we simply can only continue losing, it is just a matter of scale and frequency. Left unchecked, we will continue losing the war. What will the government and agencies do with the data at that point then?

5

HUSH PUPPIES, FLYING PIGS, GROWING TENSIONS, AND EASTER EGGS

Stuxnet, the world's first digital weapon, was disclosed in 2010 to the world. Although very much contained and only barely fully understood by many security professionals and government officials, and do not forget, the world is still coming to terms with a new norm following the 2008 financial crisis. Acknowledged as the world's worst economic disaster since the 1929 Great Depression, the 2008 financial crisis was triggered mainly by greed, mis-selling, and misrepresentation. The Federal Reserve and the Department of US Treasury were battling with Banking collapses and negative equities like never previously experienced. Unemployment in the US hit 9% and there was a general feeling that Banking Executives had effectively sold out corporate America for their own personal wealth and greed at the cost of the global economy and in particular, the average US citizen. The global economy was hit by more than just a ripple effect as government after government felt the shock waves and did all they could to shore up their own economies. One of the challenges was that some clever mathematicians helped to create a new product line and called it Mortgage-Backed Securities (MBS) and the Banks started eating them up, they simply could not get enough of them. Property prices in 2006 had already started to level and fall for the first time in decades. Fannie Mae and Freddie Mac were right at the heart of the issue and soon as part of the entire new world's financial order. It was not long before the Subprime Market was effectively bundled into the equation. People without jobs, and without much hope of getting one, were being given mortgages in sub-prime real estate, and areas en masse. The bundled MBSs were sold in their $billions but had little, to no real value, the market had acted initially as if there was a gold rush: sadly, there was no real gold but for a very few.

DOI: 10.1201/9781003204145-5

The financial crisis hit the US and the rest of the world hard and with devastating effect. During this period, the US housing market saw an average 31.8% decline, the Treasury Department spent $439.6 billion, AIG received a $182 billion bailout, and Lehman Brothers collapsed after being a globally leading Banking institution since 1847, they filed for bankruptcy in 2008. Total tax cuts and spending was $813 billion, and Fannie Mae and Freddie Mac were also bailed out to the tune of $187 billion.

At the same time as all this was going on, Stuxnet had been designed, developed, and then deployed and many $billions were spent to give the Iranians, what would turn out to be little more than a bloody nose as mentioned. It did not stop their Nuclear Programme, merely slightly delayed it at best. It had also created a new Modus Operandi that would serve to be the new MO for other Nation States and trickle down to become part of a new cyber capability and armoury, possibly not even considered much and certainly not addressed at the time. However, what the US Agencies had shown was incredible manipulation and capability that would go on to be adopted by other Nation States with nefarious intent. The biggest mistake of all this created a constant digital state of peril and constant digital conflict and US corporations, government offices, and regular companies including the Healthcare, Education, and many more were completely ignorant and ill-equipped to resist any offensive attack. They were simply unable to put up any fight and were little more than easy targets. These entities, many of them supplying the US government, including the DHS and DOD, were, and still are, nothing more than extremely vulnerable and insecure.

The cyber posturing and fight had been called on, with little to nothing to back it up defensive wise. As David Bowie said in 1999:

> The impact of the internet, for the good and the bad, is unimaginable, I think we are on the cusp of something exhilarating and terrifying. It is not just a tool, it's an alien life form (as he laughed) it is going to be so different to anything that we can really envisage at the moment. Where the interplay between the user and the provider will be so in sympatico it's going to crush our ideas of what mediums are all about.

David Bowie was most certainly not wrong; however, I suspect that no one envisaged just how rapidly both opportunities, and more so the

HUSH PUPPIES AND FLYING PIGS

destructiveness, the internet could deliver when used offensively and with nefarious purposes.

In 2011 David Cameron, the British Prime Minister was speaking at the Munich Security conference and his focus was Terrorism. He confirmed that although the UK was dealing with its own deficit, it would still meet its commitment to the 2% target for NATO on spending. He went on to confirm that the UK had the fourth largest military defence budget, however, was putting the spending to better use enabling conflict prevention. This meant addressing the new and various threats that were being faced. David Cameron stopped short of saying cyberwar, however, did confirm that the country was investing in a National Cyber Security program. We can calculate that around the same time as David Cameron was giving his speech at Davos at the Munich Security conference, plans were, and possibly already had been, drawn up for the UK's equivalent of the NSA's PRISM, XKEYSCORE, and QUANTUM INSERT programs, however with a very British twist in the code names. HUSH PUPPY and FLYING PIG were the chosen code names of two programs that were developed. These programs were designed, developed, and implemented to manipulate networks by using TLS and SSL certificates that would provide the UK with similar Network Exploitation as previously used by the NSA. This gave Government Communications Headquarters (GCHQ) access to companies, internal correspondence, and pretty much anything they wanted access to.

GCHQ is the intelligence and security organisation responsible for providing signals intelligence (SIGINT) and information assurance to the UK government, associated intelligence agencies, and the armed forces in the UK. Housed in the suburbs of Cheltenham, the Doughnut building in Hubble Road and its operatives report to the Secretary of State on all Foreign and Commonwealth affairs. GCHQ was formed on 1 November 1911. The Doughnut has around 6,000 permanent staff accompanied by multi-£billion budgets. It is fair to say that GCHQ has had to reinvent itself over the years and possibly never more so than over the last two decades. Cyberwarfare and cyberattacks are being developed at such a rate of knots and capabilities are always being challenged. This has often created oversight of basic and fundamental security as we witness and that is a globally systemic failing today. All agencies across the world have been guilty, to a greater or lesser extent, of manipulating and utilising vulnerabilities for their own intelligence gathering and gain. This has often been at the cost to many others. Microsoft vulnerabilities, for example used by billions, have been found out later to have been known and used by the NSA to exploit targets. This is said to be much less the case now, however, cannot be confirmed. The work that the team of brilliant encryption and decryption experts during World War II, namely Alan Touring and William Tutte, along with their teams had undertaken and cracked, first the Enigma machine and then Lorenz by building the Bombe, would, as part and parcel and over time, be housed centrally within GCHQ's buildings and become the epicentre for British Intelligence. Encryption and decryption could make us all safe, or all unsafe.

As we learned from Edward Snowden's revelations in 2013, HUSH PUPPY and FLYING PIG were both cloud analytic tools which worked on bulk, unselected data collection. FLYING PIG is a knowledge base for investigating TLS/SSL traffic, and HUSH PUPPY is a tool for attributing private network traffic. In simple terms, both programs manipulated TLS and SSL encrypted communication over the internet by utilising their own certificates that were being implanted into the handshake. In other words, if an email, data, or any information were sent, GCHQ like the NSA could capture and harvest the data. The implementation was simple and used a Federated approach. Using multiple cloud analytics, each produced a Query Focused Dataset (QFD). Analytics were run on a weekly basis on approximately 20 billion events. The simplicity was key and a single query in the web interface resulted in calls to multiple QFDs which in turn returned to the user in separate panels. This provided fast queries, easy to maintain modular code, and more importantly, enabled easy capability to add TLS and SSL QFDs. In basic terms, what GCHQ was doing is planting their own certificates, unbeknown to everyone in the cloud and inside organisations to gain digital access, and still do.

Much of this highly classified information came out in 2013 with the revelations by Edward Snowden. Snowden, in 2013 was nearly 30 years old, and shocked the world when he broke with protocol and the American Intelligence establishment. He revealed that the US government had been secretly pursuing the means to collect every single phone call, text message, and email. The result of these disclosures confirmed that the government had been building an unprecedented system of mass surveillance with the ability to pry into the private lives of literally every person on earth. Six years later in 2019, Snowden published his book, *Permanent Record*, and revealed, for the first time, how he helped to build this system and why he was compelled to move to expose it. *Permanent Record* is a must read and uncovers much of the myths of mass surveillance, the who is, the whys, and the wherefores. It also disclosed and confirmed programs such as FLYING PIGS and HUSH PUPPY along with illustrations, classified papers, and how they worked. Both programs had been previously exposed to an extent prior to 2013 by UK's National press.

Some years later in 2018/2019, we were driving hard the ability to gain full PKI discovery and realised as a Start Up, even with some real heavyweight and globally acknowledged security leaders onboard, that the UK is very different to the US on such matters, so much so that we seized the opportunity to engage with one of the Big 4 consulting firms. We had met with all four, however, one firm realised the huge potential to actually, 'do the job right' and have PKI controls and management working for them, and indeed their clients as opposed to fighting against them and increasing insecurity. Various regulations were being heightened including audits. Accountability by shareholders, it was quickly being realised, although rarely actioned well, that security had a huge part to play as opposed to just paying lip service. The job required being done properly as opposed to simply, as we say in the UK, putting lipstick on a pig. I personally undertook the preliminary conversations and meetings and discussed all manner of areas including, Audit, Forensics, and so on and how our PKI solution, Whitehorn® would, for the first time in history, enable visibility and therefore control what TLS and SSL certificates were on their and their client's devices. Unfortunately, as with many consulting firms, it is very much a fragmented and extended timeline without much commitment unless a client would pay first. That will hopefully change soon too. Stop and think about this for a moment before I share the heritage of Whitethorn® with you. Full visibility as NIST drives and encourages everyday as their first issue to undertake as part of their security framework. You cannot secure or protect what you do not know about and this, in every single organisation worldwide is the current situation, of course, at the delight of governments. No one knows what devices they have let alone the certificates and keys on them. It is why the agencies saw this as a massive vulnerability to utilise and spoof to gain access and gain the access that they did.

Take a laptop or a similar device, for example. It is supplied by a supposed trusted partner and unpacked for the first time. It comes preloaded and ready with a Root Store with OEM Certificate chains ready to use. That makes the setting up process easy, however, of course, you have no idea or control of what is embedded within the device, what is good, bad, expired, or even revoked. The device could be compromised from the word go, and sadly, often is. What certificates might have been revoked due to being used for nefarious purposes over the last few weeks and the device may be months old already. It might come complete with Common Vulnerabilities and Exposures (CVE) sitting within a software bundle. Sure, the device may look and feel like new, however it may be crawling with bugs and backdoors ready to take your data and share with a third party. By implanting certificates this is exactly what the agencies were doing either directly or indirectly by third-party software providers.

Back to the Big 4, a date was set four weeks out to run a full, controlled environment scan using Whitethorn® on their chosen, selected, and provided Gold Standard build laptop. Their chap said they needed four weeks to plant their 'Easter Eggs' and would be doing so in the deepest and darkest depths of the OS, binaries, and so on. Finally, on the day, my CIO, Whitethorn® and PKI expert, turned up at their offices armed just with his own regular laptop with Whitethorn® installed. The first thing he did was to connect the two devices and commence the simple Whitethorn® scan. The meeting had commenced between the Big 4 attendees and our CIO with coffees being enjoyed and a great selection of chocolate biscuits. Small talk ensued and coffees were made and shared. Some 20 minutes later, our CIO declared the scan was finished and started to share the findings.

Within 20 minutes Whitethorn® found, and evidenced, all the deeply planted 'Easter Eggs' and ten times more besides. The scan revealed over 250,000 certificate instances, expired, revoked, weak cipher (SHA-1) deprecated certificates, software issues, and third-party certificate issues which weakened and relegated their own cyber posture. There were over 20,000 unique certificates and it was clear they had little real idea of the PKI landscape and as such had

HUSH PUPPIES AND FLYING PIGS   33

limited control and management. Remember, you cannot manage what you cannot see and have no idea or knowledge of. To say they were impressed was an understatement. Their Penetration Team, Legal team, Audit team all saw incredible, numerous use cases and unique benefits. Cyber Insurance, Cyber Audits, Forensics, the list was very extensive, and they realised the global game changer position Whitethorn® could, for the first time since the inception of PKI, provide. The final party piece was when our CIO drilled down a tad further to show certificate origins, validities, issuers, and so on. This is where he found FLYING PIG certificates that had been implanted into this Big 4 software and laptop. Why might it be there, it was unquestionable who planted it, however totally unbeknown to the Big 4. They were in effect being digitally bugged and literally everything they digitally said and did, could be gathered, harvested, and acted upon. Now of course we are sensible adults and realise in our business that privacy and security are not always natural bedfellows, however it was hard not to think of the audacity and possible legality of such infiltration one's own government had initiated, and their tactics were here and evidenced right before everyone's eyes.

This FLYING PIG SSL certificate enabled data, via digital connectivity and communication, to be siphoned off and shared with the Mother Ship. No permissions, warrants, or requests were made, and it was as easy as that. We had shown the incredible capability of Whitethorn® in a controlled and closed environment and word would spread. There we were thinking this is excellent, all the hard work, including the naysayers, would pay off. We can create a partnership with massive coverage, and we can help prevent breaches and ransomware implants by ensuring organisations could control and manage their PKI for the first time. No longer would they need to run the gauntlet and be a slave to PKI and hope. Unfortunately, we did not realise quite how much discomfort the guys at GCHQ and the NSA might have towards such a new capability. In hindsight of course, Whitethorn® would spoil their fun by identifying and removing rogue certificates and making PKI housekeeping possible and therefore security and privacy far simpler. It would of course however also identify their TLS and SSL plants. At the same time, Whitethorn® could reduce cyber losses by $trillions, quite a dilemma for the agencies, and although we assisted the FBI earlier this year by identifying a Korean

DNS within the US Central voting system, which they were happy to benefit from our, and Whitethorn Shield® capability, the ranks seemingly closed following this and the Big 4 showing as well as a full internal proof of concept we would undertake at a Critical National Infrastructure client. I will cover this in detail in a later chapter.

A short note on history of Whitethorn® and how it came into being might be useful at this point. Several years ago, a NATO installation found out they had been breached due to highly sensitive data being made available on the Dark Web. Our Chief Scientist, a cryptography and data expert, is NATO cleared and due to numerous projects he and his team had worked on, was asked to review the situation. He was introduced to a colleague of mine at the time he was advising several governments. A very senior level chap who was also something of a guru in the field of cryptography and PKI. There was the usual dilemma of Buy or Build and after a very short beauty parade and scan across the main protagonists within the certificate lifecycle management (CLM) market, it became abundantly clear they would need to build. Not a single company, let alone all put together, was able to provide real discovery. Instead, in the main, one had to populate their systems with the TLS and SSL certificates they knew about and they would then be able to manage them. Discovery of all certificates, including PGP and SSH, was an impossible task even with numerous tools. CLM to this day in comparison to what is now possible with Whitethorn® is like being stuck in the DOS era by comparison. It is the same as knowing and running an insecure homepage will invite being targeted and attacked but ignoring it as surely it must be someone else's problem.

The brief was clear. It had been discovered that the breach had occurred by the use of an illegal digital certificate in a similar fashion to that used for Stuxnet. It gained access and exfiltrated data, this has become a common theme for Ransomware cyberattacks. On this occasion there was no fashionable Ransomware attachment, the attacker simply wanted the data. The certificate was unknown, uncontrolled, and unmanaged, it was simply accepted. The solution had to be able to discover, identify, analyse, validate, revoke, replace, manage, and automate these, and all certificates, not just a percentage. This ideally would include PGP and SSH keys to ensure maximum coverage and depth, and it was a tall order for sure. Do not forget, no one, not a

HUSH PUPPIES AND FLYING PIGS

living person had this capability or knew what their real PKI landscape truly looks like. I could write paragraph after paragraph on the trial and tribulations the team originally went through and how they eventually developed multi-scanning capability that has now become the new PKI Gold Standard and typically discovers more than twice, often much more, certificates than a device or system is believed to have. Suffice to say, Whitethorn® is unrivalled for discovery and that could potentially save the global economy $billions, even $trillions, it did however spook the spooks.

6
ROOT CAUSE ANALYSIS, ASTON MARTINS AND CONCORDE

What exactly is Root Cause Analysis (RCA)? You will hear many people in the Risk Management business, talk about R CA and it is critical to ascertain, and fully understand how and why things happened and how to avoid such events being repeated. As a racing man, I particularly like the analogy Carroll Shelby had when he said of the 24-hour Le Mans car race, 'it's a sprint race that lasts 24 hours. It will test you, the car and everyone's resolve. You can prepare for months, spend $millions and a single washer can cost you all.' I was fortunate enough to have lunch with the great Carroll Shelby and Roy Salvadori in 1999 at Le Mans, on the anniversary of their incredible Aston Martin win there in 1959. I was also fortunate to spend the evening deep in discussion recently with Peter Brock the original designer of the AC Dayton Cobra.

Carroll was certainly not wrong and having raced internationally for many years at top level, I can testify to his statement. In 2008 when the financial crisis was starting to bite and bite hard, unbeknown to me and most of the world, and due to the financial impact, 2008 would turn out to be my last full racing season. I had enjoyed some great success, winning the Autosport three hours, finishing on the podium several times in the Spa six hours, winning the Aston Martin Championship, the Innes Ireland Trophy, the highly prized and famed Oulton Park Gold Cup with previous winners reading like a who is who of former F1 drivers such as Sir Jackie Stewart and Graham Hill and many others. I must have been useful I guess as I also held several lap records including SPA which was acknowledged as the world's toughest circuit.

DOI: 10.1201/9781003204145-6

38   **STUXNET TO SUNBURST**

I had no regrets however in August 2008 with my young family and a crowd of several tens of thousands watching the British GT Championship at Brands Hatch in Kent, which was the previous home to epic Formula 1 races with the likes Mario Andretti, Sir Jackie Stewart, Aryton Senna, and James Hunt. We were in a support race with Heritage Racing. I had qualified on Pole with my 650 bhp Aston Martin, which was the sister car to the famous Muncher, that raced at Le Mans in the late 1970s raced by Duncan Hamilton and was built by the same team in period. The race was filmed live on Sky TV and of course, the financial crisis was pretty much on everyone's mind, even though everyone tried to push it to the back of their minds. Development of race cars is an ongoing skill and the car I was racing would have been many tens of seconds quicker in its current race trim than that of The Muncher in period. Tyre technology and brake compounds alone would make a huge difference. In racing, the question is often asked: 'how do you make a small fortune in Motor Racing; you start with a big fortune'.

We were racing on the full Grand Prix circuit that weekend, which is rarely used and out the back, was extremely fast. I had qualified by a second and a half over the next car on the grid which in Motor Racing is a substantial advantage. I felt the car, conditions, and everything else was perfectly in tune and aligned. The lights went out and I hurtled off the grid. Sector after sector setting new record times, the car was flying and by far the quickest. Lap after lap I was pulling away with reasonable comfort setting fastest lap one after another. Settling into the race after several laps, I started lapping back markers and, on this lap, I came to the brow at Pilgrims Drop, I was registering 176 mph at the speed trap, this was going to be a hell of a last race, nothing like going out on top. For those that do not know, the superbikes on the same circuit do not get anywhere near that top speed at the same speed trap. As mentioned, after more laps I started to catch up and lap more back markers. Nothing particularly new in that and a simply manoeuvre drive around and pass. It still shocks me that so-called experienced racing drivers would move offline and wave you through when everyone knows the rule is to hold line and let the faster car go round. Pilgrims Drop had been the scene of previous incidents including the 1980's crash of Johnny Herbert's F1 racing driver crashing and breaking both ankles, the run-off is incredibly limited, less than a yard in places.

ROOT CAUSE ANALYSIS, ASTON MARTINS AND CONCORDE 39

I was now fully in my stride, and my heart rate normalised, and I had lapped half the field. Anyone that has watched the film Le Mans with Steve McQueen will remember the pounding of the heartbeat at the beginning of the race, quickening to full pace when the lights go out. The adrenalin can be so strong that it can make you feel so tired, almost sleepy as the countdown starts. As I continued lapping to the delight of the large, knowledgeable, and clearly delighted crowd, nothing looks or sounds better than a classic big Aston on full charge and with the Muncher livery of white with Union Jack stripping the Aston looking resplendent. Unbeknown to me as I approached Pilgrims Drop on this lap which, as mentioned, was the fastest part of the sector and literally falls away so you hit the top of the blind drop, a car that I was coming up to lap, had literally blown its engine seconds before I got there. Remember I was doing 176 mph at that speed trap. If you have never experienced this kind of speed, it is a real rush, things slow down right in front of you, and that speed becomes the new norm. You know when you have done 70 or 80 mph and come down to 30 mph it seems like a pedestrian pace, you simply adapt to it. What you do not have is the luxury at that speed to take too long making decisions. Looking back, and replaying in slow motion, the Aston Martin I was unknowingly coming up to lap, and on my left, was in fact slowing down and coasting off the circuit. At the time I thought nothing of it as it seemed just another car I was lapping, I was completely unaware at the time because... I would all too soon discover when I was thrown into the barriers out of control. What had happened is the driver (who shall remain nameless) had grabbed the wrong gear, he had gone from fourth to third instead of to fifth when he hit the top of Pilgrims Drop instantly over revving and blowing up his engine. Just as in Project Aurora and Stuxnet, this immediately created physical damage by breaking the internal components dumping the entire, near boiling oil and contents onto the narrow circuit ready for me to hit totally unaware and at incredible speed. I was totally blindsided and unaware of the event that was unfolding yards ahead of me on the other side of the brow. I hit the oil which was very quickly followed by the barriers on the right-hand side at what must have been at 150 mph plus. Ricocheting down the Armco as a passenger in a 1,200 kg projectile with a huge 7.2 litre engine inches away from my legs, and there was next to no run-off at this part of the circuit. I finally came to rest near Hawthorns corner several hundred yards down the circuit, and trust me, I was breaking hard. I was certainly, shaken, not stirred. The doctors and officials rushed to the near totally wrecked car, and more than likely fearing the worse. The huge screens all around the circuit kept playing the incident and my family, friends, guests watched on in total disbelief, feeling nauseous, upset, and even sick to their stomach.

I was rushed to the circuits hospital without any way to communicate with my family, to be examined for internal concussion and internal bleeding checks. It is fair to say not many people walk away from an accident at such speeds and severity. When the wreckage, and what was left of this most stunning Aston race car made it back to the pits, the reality of the crash must have really hit home. The concerns that my family and friends had, was now there in front of them in a large, mangled heap. The silent questions of how anyone could survive such a crash was clearly in their minds but not spoken... As I sat, totally livid at the sequence of events and not in full receipt of the root cause for the next 30 minutes, no one knew where I was, where I had gone, and no update was being offered. All I could try and think about was what had gone wrong and the fact I would not win the race... That is a racer for you, racing is everything, the parts in between are just waiting (Steve McQueen).

After 30 minutes, I was taken back to the Pits by bike and walked down the hill to meet my family and friends. I have never seen a ghost, however that day I found out what the look on other people's faces might be like if they did. It was as if no one had ever seen me and as if I must have superpowers, how could I walk away, let alone with barely a scratch from such a colossal incident. It was a truly sad way to end my racing career, but it had certainly ended with a bang. I am forever indebted to my team for building such an incredible and safe car.

I had been lucky, although maybe I did not appreciate it at the time, as the following week in a Formula race on the very same circuit, Henry Surtees, son of racing Legend and world champion, John Surtees was killed when an accident ahead of him caused an incident, the wheel broke off, flew through the air, and hit Henry on the head, he crashed and died a few hours later. The root cause can bely the sequence of events and the reason why outcomes may be different to those expected, or desired. In a similar way, PKI can

ROOT CAUSE ANALYSIS, ASTON MARTINS AND CONCORDE 41

secure your enterprise, or, when it lacks controls and management, it can also make it totally insecure. Being in control and losing control is sometimes a very hard, and costly distinction and lesson, however, choosing neither and going with the flow, is even more dangerous, and in the world of security is never a good option.

Another great story on RCA has a somewhat sadder outcome, nevertheless, it is a story and sequence of events that happened and took the lives of those all onboard Flight 4590. On the morning of 25 July 2000, passengers boarded Air France Flight 4590 from Paris to New York and settled in for what was supposed to be an enjoyable flight on Concorde the amazing supersonic aircraft. Sadly, their flight lasted less than two minutes. Just after lift-off, the supersonic jet crashed into a hotel in Gonesse, France, killing all 109 people aboard and an additional four people on the ground.

But why did such a tragedy happen? Concorde had an impeccable reliability record. For the answer we need to fully understand and ascertain the RCA by using data and forensic information.

Five minutes before Flight 4590 took to the runway, a Continental flight had taken off headed to Newark in the US, using the same runway and had unknowingly, lost a titanium alloy strip that had been fitted several days before in a totally different country. The strip had not conformed to the manufacturer's design or fitment. Normal protocol for every Concorde flight included a full runway inspection before take-off; this was not completed (perhaps because the flight was already delayed by an hour) and as such, the strip of titanium had not been seen or removed.

During Flight 4590's take-off, the piece of this debris from that previous Continental flight, was run over by one of Concorde's wheels which cut and then ruptured one of the Concorde's left tyres. As the aircraft accelerated down runway 26R, the tyre disintegrated, and a piece of the shredded tyre struck the underside of the wing with the speed and force of a large bullet. This part of the wing was where fuel tank No. 5 resided and the force the piece of tyre hit, caused a shock wave that ultimately caused the integrity of the tank to fail and then ignite the fuel. An incredible, terribly unfortunate sequence of events that in hindsight could have, and certainly should have, been avoided. Like many catastrophes, they can cause collateral damage and human loss. We must learn from such errors and try to avoid them from happening ever again, or greatly reduce the risk. We must always address the root cause. In the world of security, often, oversight or neglect of basic security is proven to be the root cause for breaches and attacks (including Ransomware) that can most certainly be sophisticated in their code and capability, however their initial access, the root cause, is often due to oversight, negligence, and opportunism because of the organisation's clearly visible insecurity.

As previously mentioned, Project Aurora set the path and possibly the blueprint for offensive digital manipulation by enabling digital code to alter the signals sent and received by PLC/ICS of the vast diesel electricity producing generator. By doing so, the generator control was taken over and within three minutes completely destroyed. The speeding up and slowing down of the RPM thereby damaging the harmonics of the machine to destruction. Similarly, Stuxnet followed shortly thereafter causing collateral damage at the Iranian Nuclear Facility in Natanz marking the dawn of Digital Warfare and the first ever Digital Weapon.

Over the last decade or so, the world has witnessed the single largest shift in criminal activity and the largest losses to organisations and governments and loss of control. Much of this can be attributed to the fact what was once the digital capability and backdoors to select governments and agencies is now used for nefarious purposes by most of the Nation States and cybercriminals. The wider population, just like when I was in an out-of-control race car or the incredibly sad events and unfortunate passengers onboard a crashing aircraft, we were helpless to alter the outcome, we were simply passengers.

Furthermore, the rapid shift from physical, to online (digital) has seen many organisations and unfortunately, governments, agencies, and organisations, lack the knowledge, capability, time, or discipline to ensure internet facing integrity continually controlled and monitored ensuring critical security facing and connected to the internet. When this happens, and it happens all too frequently, it is like leaving your digital front door wide open in a high crime area. Our root analysis of hundreds of breaches shows that when such a situation occurs, the likelihood of being targeted and breached is compounded and the sequence of events that can then unfold, including infiltration, Ransomware, and ultimately, the loss of command and control (C2) can often be an inevitable outcome. One only must look at the breach at SolarWinds

ROOT CAUSE ANALYSIS, ASTON MARTINS AND CONCORDE 43

in December 2020, and consequential breaches, to realise how easily things can gain momentum and become out of control.

Some 30,000 domains are attacked daily and as no single enterprise has full visibility, let alone full control and management of their PKI, and that of their third-party suppliers for that matter. It is now time to demand visibility and control. Catastrophes can be avoided. Cyberattacks and service outages occur regularly, far too regularly, and in most cases, a majority have been the result of oversight or negligence. One cannot ignore the fact that some people may not be just complacent, but complicit. Security simply cannot be left to chance; it must be managed and managed full time the same as any other risk to the business. In this case however, the root cause can often be traced. How many companies can afford to lose their share, or entire business, of this year's predicted $6 trillion to cybercrime as many are running the Gauntlet and taking totally unnecessary risks.

7

THE OFFICE OF PERSONNEL MANAGEMENT AND EQUIFAX BREACHES

In 2014, it emerged that the Office of Personnel Management (OPM) in the US, the agency that looked after the records and applications of all US government's security cleared operatives, applicants, their families, friends, and all their PII data and considerably much more, had been breached. Shockingly, for nearly a year, some 22 million SF-86 forms of US government personnel had their details exfiltrated by what was later discovered to be, a Chinese Intelligence cyberattack. Of course, OPM's internet facing and connected security was suboptimal.

A pattern had started to crystalise and it became clear that the Chinese were using lessons learned from their US counterparts and stood up two domains totally in view, but without being seen. These went unnoticed by impersonating and hijacking unmanaged domains used by the OPM. They completed the domains with new digital certificates and ensured all regular visible security and then commenced exfiltrating the data. Initially the attack commenced in late 2013 by infiltrating two companies. USIS and KeyPoint were two companies that conducted various parts of the background checks for the agency. Initially the hack was determined to be confined to a part of the network that did not contain any personnel data. It was also, rather questionably, decided to allow the hackers to remain, so counterintelligence could be gained on the actual attack and attackers. A Big Bang system reset was due to be implemented on 27 May 2014 when the attackers loaded keyloggers onto database workstations.

The breach, two breaches that were linked took place over several months. The first attack was discovered in March 2014, and the second attack happened in May 2014 when the attackers were using credentials stolen from KeyPoint. It is unclear when the earlier attack

DOI: 10.1201/9781003204145-7

45

happened, however is suspected it was several months before, possibly as early as 2013. The second attack was not discovered until 15 April 2015, nearly a full year later. Forensics discovered a link and access by these government subcontracting companies. The Directors of OPM, Katherine Archuleta and Donna Seymour, resigned over the breach. Sometime later in 2017, Chinese national Yu Pingan was arrested on charges that he created and distributed the malware used in the breach. Yu pleaded guilty to conspiracy to commit computer hacking and was deported to China, where I am sure he continues his sterling work.

The first breach was known as X1 by the department of Homeland Security. The second breach was known as X2. The breach was first discovered by the United States Computer Emergency Readiness Team (US-CERT) although later this discovery was questioned by *The Wall Street Journal*. Either way, this breach and infiltration was on a massive scale of government security cleared operatives and made it a very uncomfortable position for the US government and Intelligence agencies. In later correspondence, David J. Fox of the American Federation of Government Employees wrote:

> the Central Personnel Data File was the perpetrators target and now they were in possession of every federal employee and every federal retiree. It compromised military records, veteran status, addresses, DOB, job and pay history, health insurance and life insurance, pension, age gender and race.

When the two Chinese domains were later checked, they had been registered to two names Avengers superheroes which is a trademark of Chinese hacking groups. But no one checked at the time. Controls and management are systemically poor with due diligence rarely being checked. It is nothing short of the Wild West out there on the internet and infrastructure and seemingly, few care and it continues to be the case to this day.

The US Department of Homeland Security official Andy Ozment testified that the attackers had gained valid user credentials to the systems, more than likely through social engineering. The breaches used what was termed sophisticated malware that was consistent with a Nation State. I am unsure when the first use of the term 'Sophisticated' was used, however like wood chip wallpaper used to paper over cracked walls or Artex used for undulated ceiling covering, it was most certainly used frequently. This was often immaterial if it was or not. Either way, it sounded much better than saying we were compromised due to our own oversight and negligence or even the fact we simply ignored security. I guess it also pulled the wool over the eyes of those covering or insuring breaches and higher up the chain of command. I suspect the term Sophisticated Attack originated in either Forte Mead or Cheltenham.

On average, we inform, often moving to alerting organisations, directly or indirectly through government, 3–5 organisations, sometimes even more companies each day of their insecure positions facing and connected to the internet. The list of companies is extensive and nine times out of ten we are either ignored or met with anger questioning the rationale for sharing such information. We have witnessed organisations maintain insecure homepages for years and maintaining CVEs with high vulnerabilities and then witness them get breached. It is as if the dialogue is in foreign language.

TSL and SSL digital certificates are the privileged mechanism for ensuring that secure websites are really who they say they are, they match the domain, the certificate, and the domain owner. Typically, when one accesses a secure website, a padlock is displayed in the address bar. That confirms the authenticity, data integrity, and the data encryption, this goes on automatically. Before that icon appears, the website first presents the digital certificate, signed by a root authority, that attests to its identity and encryption keys. This can, and frequently does, happen in nanoseconds. Some latency may be experienced due to local internet speeds and happens without the user's input or knowledge. However, when it says Not Secure instead of a padlock, all the above becomes invalid. The domain could be a spoof site or being used for nefarious purposes. Cyberattackers can, as they did in the recent SolarWinds breach, use a Not Secure and create their own nefarious domain and use self-signing (untrusted certs) and present them to the client during the connection phase. More times than not, the client is totally unaware and will not even check or take a second look. This is known as Domain Hijacking and Man-in-the-Middle attacks.

The OPM had received warnings many times of security vulnerabilities and security failings. In March 2015, the Office of Inspector

General reported to Congress of persistent deficiencies in OPM's information and security programs across the entire business. Interestingly, some five years later, our own research shows there are still insecure positions and numerous suboptimal internet facing and connected security issues. The lessons were clearly not learnt and continue with inadequate controls and management across their security. Sadly, this is not an unusual situation as our finding, across many sectors including, governments, healthcare, financial services, and many more continually prove daily.

At the end of the day, the OPM was initially breached due to negligently not controlling and managing their domains and their PKI. Sound familiar, it should and is reminiscent of thousands of previous infiltrations, Network Exploitation, and PKI manipulation. The 'keys' to the kingdom were all too easy to gain and the organisation even easier to breach. It was just another case of using smoke and mirrors by saying the attackers gained valid credentials to the systems instead of saying the attackers hijacked an unmanaged domain and then had domain and administration privileges. This MO was what governments had been manipulating themselves along with many other programs for over a decade, and they did not want to highlight it. At the same time, however, the agencies must have started banging their heads on how to prevent this simple and frequently sprawling attack on thousands of organisations including the OPM. It is also how SolarWinds was initially breached. It is simply unbelievable that companies of this stature and even governments themselves keep falling for this old and quite simply, simple, basic trick. However, one only has to look at the Stuxnet attack whereby various departments within the US Administration had no idea whatsoever that they, via the NSA, were actually responsible for the attack. They were thinking they had to protect themselves against the Stuxnet attack. It was only months later they were made aware that the Monster had indeed been turned against its creators and anyone else connected. The disconnect across businesses and governments is vast to this day.

Breaches have become almost daily occurrences and across all sectors. Sadly, they are almost as quickly forgotten about. Data breaches have seemingly, almost become consumables, a cost of doing business that were superseded by the next. The so-called sophisticated attacks were blamed on a Nation State. Responsibility was typically

OPM AND EQUIFAX

49

pointed firmly towards Russia or China and perversely, almost made it okay. Presidents and leaders at the time were torn between attacks being termed cyber vandalism, cyberattack, or cyberterrorism. For example, the debacle over the Sony breach whereby some 70% of all Sony's systems were effectively breached by North Korea in retaliation for their film, The Interview. The film portrayed Kim Jong-un in, let us say in a far from a natural and balanced leader, one such situation. The Administration was called in to defend and advise Sony and requested to threaten retaliation on North Korea, and although Barak Obama made an unprecedented statement saying that no organisation or government would, or should listen, or adopt a position that a Dictator demanded, it was little more than chest pumping, and little to no action was taken. The unconfirmed, but highly suspected cyber interference on North Koreas missile program by the US was considered, once again, more of a bloody nose than a knockout blow. To this day, cyber espionage is possibly wrongly, considered fair game and the first line of defence falls upon an organisation to secure, not their government. The lines are unquestionably and confusingly blurred and urgently need further definition. An example of this could be the SolarWinds breach that has clearly targeted the US government and could be considered a tad more important and damaging than 'fair game,' let alone the estimated $1 trillion costs and losses. The aftermath and retaliation will possibly require a further publication…

In 2017, Equifax was breached and attackers exfiltrated hundreds of millions of customers' records including all their Personal Identifiable Information (PII) data. Equifax is one of several reporting credit agencies that provide an overview of the financial health of most US citizens. One could say the US economic barometer. The breach sprawled across the Equifax enterprise due to totally lax security. The fallout resulted with loud, vocal accusations of negligence, corruption, and lack of leadership. A detailed report from the US General Accounting Office showed the initial infiltration was by, you guessed it, a customer website and portal (again) and due to files not being patched, the infiltration went unnoticed. There is a common term and indeed theme here. Once domain control was gained, administrator privileges were then also achieved, and the enemy was on the inside. The attackers were able to move around to other servers and due to the lack of segmentation, they were able to laterally move around and gain usernames and passwords, of course in plain text. Remember they were on the inside and had already gained Digital Trust. Imagine meeting new people in your offices, they have a security badge and are in your offices talking to other colleagues, they must be a new member of the team. In the digital world, it is all too easy for new members to appear and go totally unnoticed currently and even if they are, they have that all important digital badge already.

The attackers in the Equifax breach were then able to exfiltrate data via the compromised domain under their control and which went undetected for months due to yet another certificate issue. Equifax had allowed a digital certificate to expire several months beforehand due to the typical lack of controls and management that we constantly witness. That certificate managed and monitored devices that managed data flows. The device managing data flow and the digital certificate that provided validity, were simply not being controlled or managed. Equifax kept quiet about the breach for a month and just like executives in a recent breach, decided to unload shares in Equifax before alerting the public of the breach. I will refrain from making a personal comment here, suffice to say, I believe the SEC should certainly be able to act against such questionable trading activity. I know Class Action Lawsuits have been launched and proving negligence will be like taking candy from a baby, plausible deniability will simply not cut it here and should never even be paid lip service to.

I am sure I do not need to highlight the breaches and sequence of events that have unfolded over the last decade. The theme of access gained via the internet and domains and the lack of, or manipulation of, digital certificates is all too common. There will also be reference throughout this book of the critical importance to make sure PKI is working for you and providing security as opposed to working against you and creating insecurity. In recent correspondence with our own UK Agency, we have urged an immediate roll out of education of security facing and connecting to the internet and PKI. We have also pointed out that it may be a tad like Turkeys voting for Christmas, however unless there is a real change and a changing of tact from dissuading and discouraging the assurance of internet security and PKI, breaches will continue to increase both in terms of frequency and severity. The NCSC Technical Director was not convinced by our findings and hypothesis... It was particularly interesting when I requested, he reviewed a research paper on several UK-based domains and the invalidity of the certificates that had expired months beforehand. He was not overly concerned by some of the Common Vulnerabilities and Exposures (CVE) but acknowledged the urgent issues with the expired, insecure, unauthenticated, and unencrypted domain due to the invalid and obsolete certificates. He said, 'if that were a government domain, I would be asking serious question and taking action.' It was at that point I confirmed it was an NCSC domain.

It was particularly pleasing this week to see the launch of the NSA paper on Eliminating Obsolete TLS protocol configurations on the back of my colleagues' ongoing dialogue and the work we are driving forward. In addition to our research and findings, it has been confirmed that SolarWinds and Malwarebytes breaches were both due to manipulation and negligence of TLS and SSL certificates, I am sure the Technical Director of the NCSC is completely aware. I will not wait for his call.

8
MARRIOTT AND CYBER INSURANCE: A FRAGILE PROP

Marriott International is an American multinational hotel chain that manages and franchises a portfolio of Hotels. Originally founded by J. Willard Marriott in 1927 and now managed by his sons Bill Marriott and Arne Sorenson, Marriott is by far the world's largest hotel group. It has 30 different brands, over 7,500 properties, and is in more than 130 countries. Boasting over 1.5 million rooms, it is fair to say Marriott is a huge organisation with revenues more than $20 billion and employs some 175,000 employees.

Marriott opened its first hotel, the Twin Bridges Motor Hotel, in Arlington, Virginia in 1957 and their second hotel, the Key Bridge Marriott, in the Rosslyn district also in Virginia. In 2012, Bill Marriott, at the age of 80, passed the CEO baton over to Arne Sorenson whilst becoming the Executive Chairman.

The Marriott World Trade Centre Hotel was destroyed in the 11 September attack in New York due to the collapse of the World Trade Centre North and South towers in the terrorist attacks. In 2020, Marriott undertook a major restructuring of many Senior Living serviced communities and their distribution services to enable focus on the Hotel Chain. It also sold off Ramada International Hotels in 2004. In 2005, Marriott set up The Vacation Club International. Marriott also contributed $250k to George W Bush's second inauguration as one of the 53 organisations to do so. There were numerous further changes made over the coming years.

On 3 October 2014, the US Federal Communications Commission (FCC) fined Marriott $600k for unlawful use of Wi-Fi monitoring system and deliberately interfering with client-owned networks. The system interfered with mobiles by forwarding fraudulent Wi-Fi de-authentication packets. This incident drew unfavourable publicity to Marriott charging guests up to $15 per day for their Wi-Fi

DOI: 10.1201/9781003204145-8

54   STUXNET TO SUNBURST

connections which would be routinely added to their guest's invoices accruing some $2.25 billion of incidental fees annually.

There were numerous acquisitions and changes over the coming years; however, by far one of the most substantial and important was the Marriott acquisition of Starwood which was finalised on 16 November 2015 and was completed on 12 May 2016. Unfortunately, this acquisition, like the vast majority we witness to this day, due diligence often only scratches the surface and virtually no one considers cyber posture, cyber resilience, and current cyber position in both organisations, let alone the company being acquired and invested in. In the case of Starwood's, they had, unbeknown to either party, been infiltrated and breached earlier in 2014 and that, due to lack of security controls and management, went unnoticed until 2018, a full four years later. Once again, immediately blamed, but also later confirmed, the attack originated from Chinese State actors. At the time it was not overly obvious why, however shortly afterwards, it was confirmed that most government officials and operatives were using Marriott as the partner Hotel group and there were agreements in place. It is not known just how many guests US government ties had; however, it is not unreasonable to hypothesise that coupled with the previous OPM breach in 2014 and the theft of 22 million US Security cleared operatives, this breach substantially surpassed it in terms of numbers during this four-year period and enabled a lot of further data harvesting, cross referencing, and affirmation of PII data on security cleared personnel.

What had happened during the merger was Marriott were due to complete a new booking system. This was the intention; however, it was not ready. As a backup plan, the original Starwood booking system was used and integrated with the existing Marriott system. Due to the Starwood booking system having already being infiltrated and compromised, when it was integrated, it compromised the entire booking system of the new Marriott group and enabled the siphoning of much of the PII data from all databases. A total of 327 million records were exfiltrated along with their personal details that could be used as desired later.

It is acknowledged that the original infiltration of Starwood enabled administration privileges and enabled access to encryption keys and that enabled the data that was encrypted, to be decrypted and read in plain text. It is also known that a total of 78 critical digital

MARRIOTT AND CYBER INSURANCE: A FRAGILE PROP 55

certificates had expired some time prior to the breach, this came to light several years later. This type of attack has become very common and the reason why internet facing and PKI control and management is critical. If access and administration privileges are achieved, anything thereafter is possible as in effect, command and control (C2) can be achieved to the point one can change all user and login details and lock out the owners. Marriott, or we should say their Outsourced IT and information security providers, Accenture, flagged an unusual database query. The database query was made by a user with administrator privileges, however quick analysis revealed that the person to whom the account was assigned was not the person making the query. Someone else had gained access, unknowingly to Marriott and possibly more worryingly, to Accenture, and in effect, taken over by C2.

Post breach, investigators began scouring the system for clues, and discovered a Remote Access Trojan (RAT) along with MimiKatz, a tool for sniffing out username/password combos in the systems memory. Together, these two tools could have given the attackers control of the administrator account. It is not clear how the RAT was placed onto the Starwood server, what is clear is no one was auditing or monitoring server and internet facing security. The root cause of the breach was unquestionably a tale of oversight, negligence, and poor cybersecurity across the business and a lacking security culture. Sadly, such issues are all too common across many companies and sectors including governments. In 2019, we provided a report to a UK-based, multi-£billion Critical National Infrastructure (CNI) organisation, and by also using Whitethorn Shield®, we found no less than three Rats on one of their servers: Killer Rat, Nuclear Rat, and Xtreme Rat. The report was shared with GCHQ, and no further action was taken. The excuse via another CNI provider said, 'GCHQ said it is ok as it is a Stand-Alone server.' The fact it was connected via Imperva and facing the internet clearly had nothing to do with it then. This CNI outsourced their hosting to DNS and CDN providers, and both organisations have been breached over the last 16 months. A real wake-up call for third-party management and security. If you do not monitor and audit, you will be attacked and breached, it is just a matter of time.

We undertook a Whitethorn Shield® research program earlier this year in March when Marriott received the Information Commissioners Office (ICO) fine for £18 million GDPR fine (originally £99 million) for the original breach out of curiosity to see what improvements had been made. We found the usual array and insecurity due to lack of controls of security facing and connected to the internet. This confirmed the group were still highly susceptible to further infiltration and attacks. I wrote, and swapped emails with Arne Sorenson who replied politely, we have this area under control. I truly hope that is the case, even though our research clearly showed a totally different position, and they did not.

To date, the bottom line, Marriott has suffered limited damage and Insurances have covered much of the costs and losses. A pertinent question for Insurance companies on such situations to consider is if a client has been negligent, and continued to be so by not adhering to, or following security best practice, not ensuring security facing the internet and allowing critical digital certificates to become invalid, how can a policy and claim be met? If a driver drove an illegal car, with bald tyres or heavily, and dangerously modified, or a house with valuables left open or with the keys in the door, would the Insurer still meet any claims? I suspect not. Estimates for Cyber Insurance total revenues have quite a range and by 2021 are estimated, by Aon, to reach $730 billion. Aon also confirm Cyber Insurance is the most rapidly growing market within the Insurance sector. However, consider the fact that total losses are predicted to reach $6 trillion in 2021. One does not need to be an accountant or mathematician to calculate the massive disparity between the two figures and are not Insures in the market to make profits? There will be an awful lot of organisations that will simply neither qualify for a cyber policy once the Insurance market and indeed the parties being insured, mature and really understand what is being insured, and what it will not cover or settle if negligence is proven. Class Actions will also be more commonly taken up against Executives and Boards that continue to ignore good basic security.

This week Professor Ciaran Martin of Oxford University and former Director of the NCSC said, 'That Insurers approach to Ransomware was funding organized crime.' The Association of British Insurers (ABI) said that the inclusion in first-party policies was not 'an alternative' to organisations doing everything possible to mitigate the damage and operational risk caused by cyberattacks, but without it, victims could face 'financial ruin.' Interesting then that both the NCSC and the ABI both maintain Not Secure domains as of last night and both have been informed. There is a strong, salient message here and that is the adage of 'Prevention is much better than cure' however it often seems very few are interested in ensuring and assuring basic security measures are constantly monitored and audited. If this position was adopted, successful cyberattacks and subsequent losses would be dramatically reduced.

Furthermore, about Cyber Insurance, apart from the traditional tickbox, subjective exercise, what evidence is sought or provided when taking out, or supplying cyber cover? I personally know many Actuaries and they simply do not have enough data or experience to weight Cyber Insurance policies. Our experience confirms that if the Acquisition and ongoing management of Marriott had been undertaken, by both parties ideally, this breach could have been avoided, or at worse, identified sooner and closed immediately reducing the breach effect and scale. Equally, when a claim is made, does the cyber underwriter make a subjective decision on such any pay out? We are aware of several claims against Insures for non-settlement in contentious cases. The most famous one currently being Mondelez V. Zurich due to the attack being considered an act of war by a Nation State. Mondelez claimed $100 million as the costs to the business for the cyberattack they suffered, and Zurich have rejected the claim and payment citing an Act of War. The NotPetya (certificate-related attack) has been blamed on a Russian State-sponsored attack. Most experts agree that Mondelez has a strong claim despite NotPetya's relation to Ukraine–Russian tensions. Zurich initially offered $10 million, however soon thereafter, retracted to offer in totality.

We have views on Cyber Insurance and to ensure it is fit for purpose and that must be the case for both parties, the Insurer and the Insured. The mistakes that are often made and testimony to the culture the financial collapse of 2008 clearly demonstrated, is when salespeople's commissions are driving behaviour as was in the case of the MBS products and SubPrime market. People will sell and people will buy. It does not mean the product or service is fit for purpose or, if when the proverbial hits the fan, will support the claimant. The huge gulf between premiums and losses means the disparity will need to be made up somehow and I can see shrewd Insurers making more moves like Zurich but possibly more so to prove negligence as in the drunk car driver of homeowner that left the door open and went on vacation and was burgled. Cyber Insurance cannot be seen or treated as a Get out of Jail card to play if the inevitable occurs and the chances of doing so are greatly increased if the basics are not adhered too. There is of course a new consideration for Shareholders holding Boards responsible for ensuring the business is secure and shareholders being affected in the event of a breach. I would go so far to say that such Class Actions will have little challenge to prove security negligence as it is woefully inadequate currently and that it includes governments.

Finally, Insurers providing Cyber Insurance must be beyond reproach. They must be setting a good example of security and demonstrate that they take internet facing and connected security seriously. Insurers take PII data and premiums online whilst being non-compliant and breaching GDPR or legal privacy laws is a major own goal and yet, this is the systemic situation our research has shown at many organisations, even the ABI themselves. You cannot expect to improve security and behaviours if you are demonstrating gross negligence, it simply is unacceptable.

9

FROM BOOM TO BUST, OR FROM $3 BILLION FLOATATION TO $1 SALE IN 18 MONTHS

Travelex was the world's largest foreign exchange specialist and was the largest global non-bank wholesale foreign exchange provider. It may not be a globally recognised brand; however, this foreign exchange organisation certainly punched above its weight. The company claimed to be a market leading independent foreign exchange business. Travelex had, over their 40-year history, built a market leading retail network of specialist foreign exchange stores and developed Travelex as a trusted and widely recognised brand in foreign exchange. Their mission was to assist customers to transfer currencies, spend, and send money around the world.

The business operated across 60 countries and covered the entire value chain of the retail foreign exchange industry. In their retail business, they operated in stores in the world's top international airports, by international passenger numbers, and in major transport hubs, premium shopping malls, high street locations, supermarkets, and city centres. They had developed a network of over 1,000 ATMs at both on-airport and off-airport locations around the world and built a growing online and mobile foreign exchange platform, having achieved 800k mobile and online transactions in 2017.

Their retail activities also included the processing of VAT refunds for retail customers, the sending of remittances and other international payments. Travelex's wholesale and outsourcing focused on the preparation, processing, and delivery of foreign currency orders for virtually all major UK banks and, increasingly, international commercial banks, as well as for travel agencies, hotels, and casinos. They sourced and distributed large quantities of foreign exchange banknotes for customers,

DOI: 10.1201/9781003204145-9

including central banks and international financial institutions. Their presence across the entire value chain supported their ability to identify and secure business opportunities and provide bespoke product and service solutions to their customers. All in all, a great organisation that provided an incredibly useful service to their clients and the entire Financial Services industry.

In 2014, Apax Partners sold its majority stake of 51% to UAE-based Indian businessman B. R. Shetty valuing the company at approximately £1bn. Shetty also owned the UAE Exchange, a UAE-based money transfer business. The acquisition was supported by Abu Dhabi-based investment vehicle Centurion and completed the acquisition in January 2015.

In May 2019, Travelex, the UAE Exchange and a number of other financial service businesses operated by B. R. Shetty were placed into a holding company called FINABLR, which was as part of a major IPO on the London Stock Exchange that took place on 15 May that year. By mid-2019, FINABLR began co-branding the businesses within its estate.

As with many companies, FINABLR, and indeed Travelex themselves, business was business and security was often seen a necessary evil and was certainly not their focus. More a cost of doing business and an inconvenience, besides, who on earth would want to attack a company with hundreds of $millions of cashflow (in physical cash) and links to literally every Financial Services organisation?

On 31 December 2019, only months since their IPO valuing the company at around $3 billion, and a year ago on this very day of writing, Travelex announced they had been breached by cybercriminals demanding a Ransomware payment of £5 million. The cybercriminals had gained access to, and exfiltrated around 5GB of data and encrypted and possibly copied it implying PII data was also taken. Record profits had been enjoyed since the IPO and now they were receiving a major blow, but why and how?

Two days after the announcement, on 2 January 2020, we researched the breach and immediately discovered that Travelex's main website, their homepage, was Not Secure. This meant that it had no certificate due to the digital certificate unknowingly expiring or it had been misconfigured. This meant the domain was extremely vulnerable and indeed, made itself a target to cybercriminals using

FROM $3 BILLION FLOATATION TO $1 SALE IN 18 MONTHS 61

OSINT capability. We wrote to Travelex's CEO Tony D'Souza and the security team immediately. Several emails we also wrote to FINABLR and Mr Shetty himself alerting them to our findings for fear of further attacks, but to no avail. Several weeks later, we finally did get a response, from a highly embarrassed member of the security team member who acknowledged the certificate issue and confirmed he had issued a new certificate on the domain. Sadly, the negotiated £2 million Ransomware payment had been already been paid and the spread of malware had already started some months earlier. It is simply too little too late.

Travelex closed their websites during the early stages of the breach, the company initially claimed it was due to planned maintenance. But after several days, the picture emerged of how this 'simple' mistake had left the company vulnerable to attack. The criminals maximised the domain's vulnerability, infiltrated it, knowing they would go undetected and gained access to the company's Virtual Private Network (VPN), provided by Pulse Secure. The vulnerability made it then possible to access a vulnerable network without a valid username or password, switch off multi-factor authentication, and view logs and cached passwords in plain text. This gave cybercriminals the opportunity to attack Travelex with Sodinokibi Ransomware. This then allowed them to encrypt Travelex's files so the company could not access them, it is believed that copies of personal data (PII) for thousands of its customers were also taken.

While the vulnerability was ultimately catastrophic, the fault for the Travelex attack did not lie with the software; Pulse Secure had identified and patched the vulnerability in April 2019. The fault lay with Travelex itself: It had failed to apply the patch to its own servers, leaving itself unnecessarily vulnerable for over eight months. We can only speculate; however, we believe the vulnerability and obsolete TLS/SSL maintain the Travelex homepage, was Not Secure during the company's IPO. This would lead to very questionable due diligence and a woeful understanding of basic security from all parties involved in the IPO including Travelex, all Investors, and LSE themselves.

In April 2020, Travelex's auditors PWC took over the day to day running of the Travelex's business as Administrators and laid off over 3,000 staff and closed outlets. There was also an announcement and disclosure by Travelex's chairman on 18 August 2020, of a missing

$billion in accounts. On 29 December 2020, FINABLR, owned by businessman B. R. Shetty, sold its operations to Global Fintech Holding AG (GFIH), an affiliate of Prism Group AG of Israel for the sum of $1.

We cannot comment on the business dealings of FINABLR, however can confirm that the MO for this attack and breach and many others is they are being targeted, infiltrated, and then breached due to inadequate security facing and connected to the internet. This is very similar to the December 2020's SolarWinds's breach, and many more, in as much that insecure domains facing the internet are being flagged up to anyone and everyone willing to subscribe to the service. That includes cybercriminals. Criminals have no qualms whatsoever of going further and breaching the Computer Misuse Act (CMA). These are criminals let us not forget, nameless, faceless criminals with one goal. OSINT reports can show software issues, server issues, and subdomains. One access point is all that is required, and these can be found literally in their millions. OSINT technology was originally developed to provide the service and capability for organisations to ensure they are secure and have not missed a security issue facing the internet. Unfortunately, cybercriminals are clearly much better at using OSINT to discover insecurities than the good guys are at providing security as our research continuously shows that major organisations such as government, DOD and DHS supply chains, Healthcare, Fortune 500, and many more organisations overlook, leave, or are negligent when it comes to ensuring that their domain ecosystems are secure and managed correctly.

Subdomain hijacking is unquestionably a major factor, possibly even the major factor as to why we are witnessing breaches every day and the reason each cyber gang, State Sponsored or otherwise, have thousands of people in their teams sitting in warehouse-type buildings looking to gain access to 30,000 plus websites a day. Think about it for a minute, if you were a cyberattacker and based five thousand miles away from your targets, you've a laptop or PC and your goal is to infiltrate a target, you do not care which target. What is the first thing you do? Of course, you see if there are any vulnerabilities across their domains. This is not rocket science and people really need to wake up to the fact. If they connect to the internet and maintain a Not Secure position, they make themselves, and their clients and

FROM $3 BILLION FLOATATION TO $1 SALE IN 18 MONTHS 63

connected organisations a target. By virtue of being insecure they also inadvertently publicly declare that security is not a priority for their company. One look inside will, often, show a series of additional vulnerabilities and a breach opportunity in waiting. A disparate set of domains, servers, and outdated technology, lacking controls, and management, it is a cyberattacker's dream. The sad part is this is everywhere, a criminal can find access at every turn, they simply cannot reel in or infiltrate their victims quickly enough. The criminal part is that organisations are simply not addressing these basic and fundamental security issues. Companies are spending $millions on having the latest bells and whistles and the next best thing that their peers all have, but often totally ignoring internet facing and connected security. This area, as we know, will topple the house and has done in recent, high-profile breaches. Cybercriminals will delight in the fact that thousands of clients, including governments, will be breached too no matter what bells, whistles, or spends they have made, it will certainly be their bragging rights and then they move onto the next, connected target. Spend $1 or $100 million on security but ignoring this area means you have simply wasted your budget.

10

DID SOMEONE SAY CRITICAL NATIONAL INFRASTRUCTURE AND NUCLEAR POWER

In late 2019, I was delighted to accept an invitation to the Swiss Embassy in London to attend the Swiss Embassy Cybersecurity, closed security conference, and would be meeting some known, and some unknown members of the security fraternity and community. Whitethorn® and its heritage has an affinity with the Swiss, so it was a pleasure to attend again. On the day of the event, I met many of the hundred or so attendees and due to Chatham House rules cannot provide details of attendees, however, can confirm they were all distinguished, senior security professionals. Drones, semi, and fully autonomous vehicles were among the topics high on the focus of the event. General communications, including 5G, along with the need to drive full control, visibility, and management were topical subjects also. Public Key Infrastructure (PKI) was not a major topic, however every single element of the event and the events were totally reliant upon PKI. The general, global increase in attacks and successful cyberattacks was also a focus that required immediate action and remediation.

The panel consisted of industry leading figures and organisations who worked and supplied both the domestic, but more so in the military sectors. Critical National Infrastructure and the commercial space were also present. The questions during the presentation were both pertinent and very insightful. The audience and presenters were indeed highly knowledgeable and focused within their subject matter. I met with the Swiss Ambassador again and was introduced to the panel at the after-drinks event in the Ambassador's private residence. I thoroughly enjoyed two conversations with one of the senior Ministry of Defence (MOD) chaps and another that ran technology for a particular CNI organisation.

DOI: 10.1201/9781003204145-10

During the meetings I took time to speak with both on our unique PKI technology, and its critical importance to every and all facets of security. The conversations were kept at a reasonably high level and we agreed to discuss further, and in more depth in separate, follow-up meetings. The following day I emailed both and received almost immediate replies requesting further information along with a meeting date. It is fair to say at this point that both individuals and organisations had an extreme interest, but not an in-depth knowledge of PKI and the entire spectrum of security's reliance upon it. Over the next week or so, we agreed to meet and discuss further, including a Proof of Concept (PoC). We met with the CNI organisation in their offices and agreed a PoC along with a scoping program.

The meeting with the MOD confirmed that all security and technology was outsourced to third parties, however the chap also confirmed that there was a huge desire to enable better controls internally and externally and that included internet facing which our initial reports showed was far from ideal. With suboptimal domains and subdomains, the MOD was in fact woefully insecure. I was then introduced to the Global third-party company who managed the MOD's technology and security. With contract values in the hundreds of £millions annually, the company was reasonable to assume that the contracts were of extreme importance. More on that meeting later, however as a precursor, we ran Whitethorn Shield® on their internet facing domains, and these were also found to be suboptimal and insecure. No one was immune or doing a particularly good job in this critical area.

The CNI's PoC was originally scheduled for February 2020 and was moved twice due to the CNI team's availability, constraints, and timing. On the eve of the onsite PoC, Covid-19 created uncertainty and travelling for a three-day, onsite PoC, including flights from Munich, hotel rooms, and trains journeys, it was decided with the client, that we would set up remote capability instead of getting our Chief Scientist in from Germany with restrictions looming. Our CTO and CIO would come down from central England and I would be driving some 300 miles to the site. I was rather peeved with Marriott for not refunding a penny for the three days and four rooms that had to be cancelled given the lockdown situation.

The team worked brilliantly and provided an alternative and that was to upload Whitethorn® under the care of the designated CNI's professional Project Manager, onto their Gold Standard laptop and for us to run the scans remotely working closely and congruently with their team. It was, as expected, more labour-intensive and more time-consuming. We had to deal with certain technical issues and addressed them due to the first remote use of Whitethorn®, however the PoC was undertaken and completed, the data gathered and loaded onto the client's private portal which was being exclusively used for this analysis. The PoC was to cover several selected and agreed devices including servers, laptops, phones, etc. The three-days onsite by our team of four ended up being spread over a few weeks, however, multiple scanning of the target devices was manged professionally and managed by the CNI's PM and his onsite team. It took a short time to identify numerous, concerning issues across what would be less than 1% of all the client's devices across their global enterprise. The PoC was to be concluded by the presentation of a full report of the research and findings, some of the findings at source were so concerning and presented such vulnerability that it was impossible not to inform the CNI at source. In the main we tried to refrain from discussing too many vulnerabilities until the scanning was complete.

Once completed, the report was carefully put together and turned out to be a comprehensive, 41-page document covering all findings across the entire PKI of the devices in scope. Suffice to say we researched internet facing security which at the time was solid, however researching again in November 2020 showed considerable high vulnerabilities which confirmed a lack of ongoing controls and management in the organisation so far as internet facing security goes. The report went into detail of PKI vulnerabilities, certificate validity, encrypted keys, algorithms, fake/test certificates, keystores, root certificates, and included incredibly concerning untrusted root certs found, self-signed certificates, public and private keys, certificates from sanctioned countries, and so on. It is important to remind the reader that this organisation is a Critical National Infrastructure company that supplied numerous sectors including the MOD and Nuclear. It might be worth mentioning that in their offices on the first meeting was a chap who in the industry is affectionately known as a 'Double Hatter' and worked for a government tied supplying company and GCHQ. That is quite normal.

Some of the findings are as follows:

Weak keys	(non-compliant with several governing bodies)
Excessive private keys	(easily manipulated to take C2)
Fake/test certificates	(often a sign of infiltration and plants)
Default credentials used for keystores	(major red flag)
Deprecated algorithms	(major red flag)
Untrusted root certificates	(major concern, keys to the kingdom)
Suspicious software	(often hiding malware)
Revoked certificates	(totally untrusted environment and revoked for a major reason)

These above findings would alone have any security professional panicking and ensuring the team were burning the midnight oil to address and remediate; however, there was more, much more.

Specifically, Whitethorn® had discovered, across the target devices in scope the following:

19 unique revoked certificates (1 is 1 too many and can enable C2)

Eight keystores with default credential (a huge no no)

Untrusted root certificate (some call this game over)

22,512 expired certificates (major concerns, what did they use to do and what did they authenticate? What no longer worked as a result)

3,000 SHA-1 certificates (deprecated in 2011 so already ten years out of date and enables easy exploitation and further creates major vulnerabilities)

78 certificates due to expire in the next 30 days (control and management however not aware)

2,186 certificates with validity for over ten years (a big danger, cert validity has legally been enforced and reduced to two years)

603 weak key lengths (need strengthening)

535 certificates expiring within three months (controls and management however unaware)

Microsoft Windows Crypto API vulnerability (major vulnerability unpatched)

Over 400 Russian, Chinese, Korean, Taiwanese suspicious certificates were found that also presented vulnerabilities and required

CNI AND NUCLEAR POWER

further investigation (major vulnerabilities and legally questionable, such findings could imply Nation State infiltration and exfiltration of IP and PII data. Remember this is a CNI and Nuclear organisation).

Our final comments on the research, findings, and report confirmed that numerous, serious, and highly vulnerable implications had been identified that posed serious cybersecurity and insecurity implications that if they had not already been compromised, they certainly could easily be, which could have serious implications and undoubtedly, posed a National Security concern.

The comprehensive and extensive report was presented to the team at the CNI and due to still being under Covid-19 restrictions, a call was arranged between our contacts and their security leadership. Of particular note at this stage, it is important to point out that their CISO was quite a new recruit and had a limited technical background, a limited knowledge of PKI, and clearly had not requested the scanning and visibility of their PKI. I appreciate he may have felt as if he had been thrown in at the deep end. The report clearly identified and confirmed the number of issues along with the issues themselves. The report did not however show where the issues were apart from the fact, they had been discovered within the target devices as part of the original scope and would require Whitethorn® to identify and indeed remediate. It would be all but impossible to repeat the exercise let alone across the remaining 99% of the enterprise. Remember, Whitethorn® was developed to discover and remains unmatched and unrivalled in this area.

Whilst the report was being compiled, I was introduced to another CNI in April 2020, and we provided a Whitethorn Shield® report to them. This company is another global CNI providing services across the UK, US, and many other countries including military and governments. Once our research was finished, we presented the findings to their CISO (ex-CISO of the first CNI coincidentally) who immediately and literally fell off his chair. There sitting on one of the internetfacing servers, were no less than three Remote Access Trojans (RATs), Nuclear, Killer, and Xtreme RAT. All are well-known for their corrosive and intrusive capabilities and known to be used extensively by cybercriminals to capture data and gain access. The CNI confirmed they were unaware and would deal with the issue. Several weeks later the issue had not been dealt with however it was discovered that the hosting provider, Imperva, the DNS had been breached in late 2019, several months earlier, and Digicert, a leading Certificate Authority was also breached, possibly because of Imperva's earlier breach. Digicert was breached in May 2020 with ongoing implications due to thousands of issued certificates to their clients. Consequential effects of such breaches cannot be played down as CAs, DNS, and CDNs must provide total digital trust, sadly this is rarely the case.

Back to the first CNI, our client, the report and conference call took place between my team which consisted of my CIO, my CTO, and myself and the CNI team and the new CISO. After very brief introductions, the new CISO said: 'You are making some very strong accusations here, and I will be gentle with you' to which my contact sent me a text stating he was surprised by the tone of their CISO and clearly his manner was unnecessarily aggressive in nature. As mentioned, their CISO did not request the PoC and possibly felt a tad threatened although he had no need to be. I retorted immediately and confirmed that we were not making any accusations, we were providing and presenting the facts from the PoC and report that we were commissioned to provide. The call went on for a short while and my contact, who was clearly very embarrassed by the tone and style of the security teams conduct and wanted to get to the point that confirmed the unique capability of our company and Whitethorn® offered as the PoC and report had demonstrated. This point was eventually reached, and it was confirmed from our side that, given the findings, an urgent audit and review along with a wider program using Whitethorn® should be undertaken across the entire business especially given the National Security implications of our findings. The CNI acknowledged and confirmed they would get back to us.

Following the conversation, it seemed we may be speaking in a different language. We had highlighted the major areas of concern (grave concern) with reference to the report and findings. The findings were never challenged or questioned by any individual or person at any stage. We were positive that the CNI would want to, in fact need to engage and engage quickly due to the findings and to ensure cybersecurity across the business was indeed effective and to confirm no infiltration or further infiltration was possible. Given their CNI position and Nuclear capability, it was of course

CNI AND NUCLEAR POWER

something that most certainly could not be ignored, especially as they also provided cybersecurity services to a large clientele as part of their overall services. At the time, I was unaware, however the CNI had just finished pulling its auditing together with a Big 4 and was producing their Annual Accounts for public disclosure. The timing and acknowledgement of our report could not be anything but incredibly negative and could not be mentioned. As a footnote, there may be shareholder implications and further responsibilities to consider by non-disclosure and inactions on findings down the line.

Throughout the PoC, my contact confirmed that he had a budget of several hundred £million to bring on technology that they could benefit from directly and that they could also take to their clients. He sent a text message confirming he wanted the CNI to work exclusively with us to provide the CIP and Whitethorn® services to their government clients. My contact confided in me by saying that he wished he could invest in our company personally.

A further two weeks or so elapsed and we finally heard from the CNI confirming they were grateful for the report, however, and rather sheepishly, we were informed the CNI would not be asking for any further work from us. We were more than a tad surprised and rather concerned given their incredibly insecure position with Russian and Chinese presence as just two major areas of concern. As mentioned, it would be an impossible task for the CNI to address and remediate all the findings of the report let alone even tackle the remaining 99% of the enterprise. It would simply need to be ignored and left insecure, which is how it remains to this day. There would be zero control or management of their already woefully insecure PKI. The conversation continued and I informed my contact that as a matter of National Security, we could not simply ignore the findings, especially given the Chinese and Russian identified presence, and the real and present danger and possibility of command and control (C2) being taken over.

My contact became very agitated and demanded he be informed if I was going to the press, he was acting totally out of character, and in my opinion, he was clearly extremely concerned. Given their annual reports would be adversely affected let alone future multi-£billion contracts, I could understand why. I assured him that was not my intention, however, it was to escalate the situation to the CNI Board as the magnitude and severity of the findings warranted more attention than had been received by their newly appointed nervous CISO. Sure, the CISO may have inherited a poor cybersecurity position; however, for the first time ever globally we were providing PKI visibility. My contact immediately apologised for his outburst and confirmed that he still believed 100% in our company and Whitethorn® capability and what we had uniquely developed and our capability, but his hands were tied and was truly sorry. He also confirmed that his accelerated education on cybersecurity was down to our personal relationship over the months and that he had been unquestionably well educated, for which he was extremely grateful.

There are two types of security experts, ones that roll over and tick boxes and are in the majority, then there are those that simply do not just roll over even when they know that a 'cover up' is taking place. Ask no questions and you will get paid each month. Security is the same. You can tick boxes and leave front doors wide open. When the likes of Senators and Committees review, they simply do not know and can happily sign off $billions for more Zero Days, and frequently do.

Suffice to say, it is abundantly clear where I sit on this, there is one way or no way, so I prepared to take on the Board, I did not realise I would be taking on the 'establishment' in the doughnut and UK government. However, I approached several Board members and specifically a known knighted member and the COO who both were rather surprised and unaware of the PoC or the report. Although both were made aware at a later stage of our involvement (just), they were not aware of any of the specifics. So much so that after deliberating and swapping several emails and exchanges, requested permission to share the report with GCHQ. Of course, originally, I was thrilled and delighted by this outcome. GCHQ's lead security for the UK, and would surely, unquestionably be as shocked and concerned by damning and highly vulnerable position that this CNI was in, and also the implications to National Security that the Whitethorn® scanning and research had shown. They would surely be thrilled to gain such Actionable Intelligence. There was no way in a million years the CNI could be allowed to ignore such deeply concerning and compromising findings and GCHQ would call in the cavalry. As Whitethorn® is our proprietary technology, there was no way Whitethorn® capability could be substituted no matter how many tools you have. A previous Barclays Bank's CISO had recently called Whitethorn® after seeing

CNI AND NUCLEAR POWER

it in action, 'The Truth Serum' it stuck, and I liked it. There was nowhere to hide TLS or SSL certificates no matter what state they were in or why they were and hiding, or possibly, a point we had not considered enough at the time, who had planted them…

After a further two weeks with no further communication, the double shock that then befitted us when, again, no denial or questioning of the findings, we were informed by the CNI that GCHQ had advised them, an MOD contractor and Nuclear provider among many other things, not to undertake any further PKI discovery and effectively, leave their PKI in the same, highly vulnerable and compromised position, which also meant ignoring all the findings and Russian and Chinese discoveries. The penny dropped as it dawned upon us, it is not our technology, company, our capability, or the cut of our cloth, put simply although we were discovering everything, warts and all that could cause breaches, take out Power Stations, shut down banks, national infrastructure, and even government, it was the fact we would also uncover all the government TLS and SSL plants. The same plants had illegally been deployed and inserted as part of Computer Network Exploitation without permission, sanction, or knowledge. So, it was easier to say thanks, but no thanks. Who is going to go against the government and their intelligence agency? Perversely, this is a major reason today's IT and security teams do not have a good understanding and appreciation of the serious, critical implications of getting PKI wrong, they have, and continue to be encouraged, and paid, not to understand.

Agencies around the world face a huge dilemma and crossroads right now and are clearly unsure what to do about it. Whilst the world metaphorically burns down due to the constant cyber fear and cyberattacks which are almost impossible to keep track of, the collusion, the dirty secrets the agencies keep that maybe some have suspected, but few can confirm, is that their Network Exploitation and TLS/SSL manipulation capability is now in the hands of our adversaries. Security experts that are now in the front line and tasked to protect, simply lack the skills or knowledge to protect and secure themselves, let alone their clients including governments. The incredible dilemma is to either finally come clean and out of the shadows before there are no companies or governments left that have not been infiltrated, and breached, or stay quiet and keep blaming China, Russia, North

Korea, and so on. Ultimately agencies need to realise they are not able to fight their way out of the mess, a mess they created with little to no consideration under the auspices of security. Instead of trying to continue to maintain monopolies and stock pile Zero Day offensive capability, in their vain attempt to bulldozer security which is simply inadequate, agencies need to embrace new technologies, not because they secretly invested or have control, but because the new technologies can genuinely make a difference, provide real security, and reduce cyber breaches and losses.

11
CYBERATTACK FATIGUE

January 2020 seemed to be a wash with breaches, even more so than normal and in truth, upon further investigation, it was hardly surprising. The combination of continued and systemic poor security coupled with the holiday season makes for a cybercriminal's perfect, seasonal cocktail. The UK-based Budget airline company, easyJet in addition to Travelex, suffered a major breach that also saw the exfiltration and compromise of several million customers' PII Data. It was not until a few months later that the breach was made public in April 2020. Even though a major consulting cybersecurity firm and the NCSC were both involved from the outset in January, the breach would not be made public knowledge until several months later. Both the consulting firm and the NCSC were actively involved from the outset of the breach occurring in January. It was considered wise not to advise of the breach until the actual events were better understood.

I recall at the time in April when we the public were made aware of the breach, our research team started their research and as always looked at the internet facing security and numerous domains of easyJet. Quite frankly they were horrified to discover a high percentage, more than 50% were running suboptimal and totally insecure connected internet facing sites. In other words, numerous subdomains were maintained as being Not Secure. Incredibly this included the domain being used to notify shareholders and the public by way of breach updates www.corporate.easyjety.com. A typical case of building and launching websites, capturing, and sharing data but neglecting to consider their customer's ongoing security and their PII data, treating it as a commodity thereafter. Very much a case of sell as much as you can through the wonderful (not so new) digital medium and internet and simply glossing over security. Even the notice of the breach, like Travelex's only weeks before, was hosted on a Not Secure website which is nothing short of a totally shocking schoolboy error.

DOI: 10.1201/9781003204145-11

Maybe everyone is guilty of demanding cheaper prices and due to the internet, seemingly being a lower cost of sales, indirectly encouraged and allowed poor management of security on a global scale, that is the polite version, the reality is there is absolutely no excuse.

We wrote email after email including sharing examples. I also personally sent and swapped emails with easyJet's founder and still largest shareholder, the charismatic Sir Stelios Haji-Ioannou, to cease the haemorrhaging continuing due to the continuing oversight and ongoing insecure position. It was at this time it became all too apparent that there was a rather fraught in house wrangle and a call for the Board to be dismissed by the shareholders. As such the insecurity continued confirming that perimeter security and defences were still not being considered an issue several months after the actual breach. This continued as a major threat for further cybercriminal infiltration. This made absolutely no sense at all especially with senior cyber experts assisting along with the NCSC, what was being done? Surely not another case of watching the attackers.

There are moves for a multi-£billion Class Action lawsuit against easyJet as the number of customers' PII data being taken in contravention of GDPR regulations are in their millions. In fact, the initial case has commenced and being considered and calculated on a per capita fine and claim. This figure has over the last ten years moved from almost pennies to £thousands per claimant. Having said that, the breach BA suffered in 2018 whereby less than 500,000 peoples' PII data was stolen due to another Shadow website (BAWays.com) being stood up and inserted into the ecosystem, and that caused, for a total of only six days, people were being diverted, booking and buying their flights, online via the spoof BA website. The original fine the ICO said they would levy was £183 million, however that has recently been vastly reduced to £20 million, in our opinion an incorrect decision almost making security negligence acceptable as a cost of doing business. Add the confusion on Insurance and the lines are anything but defined. There is a clear distinction between regulatory fines and Class Actions lawsuits. The latter can also include Shareholders taking Class Actions if a company and its Board are suspected of security negligence. If a breach is experienced and a fine levied for non-compliance, chances are strong for both clients and shareholders. The case is made all the stronger if it can be proven to have occurred due to security negligence and misleading investors and allowing customers to become vulnerable. There are several such cases that are currently in the courts and sadly, it is always relatively easy to prove negligence.

Both the examples of Travelex and easyJet show that inadequate internet facing security, controls, and management of domains were the initial access, root cause if you like was the point of infiltration. I would like to confirm that both have addressed this, critical area, however I am afraid I cannot. Two relatively new terms are being used, and all too frequently: Breach Fatigue and Sophisticated. Some executives are simply not considering or understanding that defence in depth, starting at the perimeter, is critical if they are ever to achieve security, any security. They may hear the term sophisticated which can mean highly skilled and crafted, or simply be a better term that tries to disguise negligence. In these two breaches, and thousands more, yes thousands, the initial targeting was due to open visibility of security negligence and competency. The initial infiltration is due to negligence and thereafter, the Malware, Ransomware, Worm, call it what you wish, can and often is purchased literally off the shelf on the Dark Web as a product or service to be used once access has been gained. Various types of malware and Ransomware and various variants are usually in a cybercriminal's tool bag and armoury. First, they simply need access or the belief that access is possible. This is clearly demonstrated by poor maintenance and insecure websites and unfortunately is all too frequent. One US missile manufacture has been insecure since 2013, so nearly eight years. Our three emails to their executives have fallen on deaf ears and yet they could, due to their existing Digital Trust, provide the access to the DOD, DHS, and government. Rarely do we see worse especially in a highly secretive and often mission critical situation.

Without being too candid, I would say that what is known, what is done, and what should be done has such a vast disparity and that insecurity is systemic across Nations and organisations. Even Health organisations that pay Ransomware, and that could be considered to have effectively facilitated the breach due to their negligence in the first place, and by maintaining a Not Secure homepage, pre and post breach, are nothing short of committing and facilitating further breaches and supporting organised crime. Such actions can unquestionably be considered complicit by their actions, or their inaction to shore up the defences. I have written four times to their CEO after connecting on LinkedIn and still, several months later they remain Not Secure even though all the messages have been read. Maybe they have other motives for leaving the business open to further, future breaches. Any company being this negligent demonstrate total lack of client's data security and why fines are being rightly levied. It would be good if the ICO and the SEC would take such breaches by companies more frequently and more seriously. In the first six months of 2020, some 8 billion personal records PII data had been compromised, that is the equivalent of every man, woman, and child in the world today. When did you last hear of a cybercriminal being imprisoned?

Moving neatly onto the medical sector, we undertook research using Whitethorn Shield® across the US on the top 1,000 Health Sector providers. Following the Anthem breach on 4 February 2015, it was clear that the Health and Health Insurance sectors were far from secure and did not take security too seriously. The Anthem breach suffered the initial theft of over 37 million personal files and PII date, this number increased to over 78 million. By way of an apology, Anthem, out of their generosity and guilt, kindly offered free credit monitoring... Our research collated the details of the worse 200 Healthcare operators and showed a systemic failing across a very high percentage of organisations with insecure and compromised domains. Many had already been breached and many were completely insecure and highly vulnerable to breaches. Software, server, outdated CVEs were the norm just as was in our research across the US States as part of our research pre the 2020 Elections.

Understandably, Health Centres, Missile manufactures, Health Insurance, and Airlines are not, by their very nature, overtly focused or competent when it comes to being experts within the field of security, however as Steve Jobs so eloquently said, 'It doesn't make sense to hire smart (security) people and tell them what to do, we hire smart people so they can tell us what to do' and this is where the problem starts. Security people, in the main, know that perimeter security and connecting to the internet means you are benefitting from that connectivity, however if you ignore internet facing and connected security, it will cost you many times over. It is estimated that in 2021 online spending will be eclipsed by losses via with a ratio of 2:1, in other words, for every \$ spent, \$2 will be lost to cybercrime. Make no mistake, these losses will and are causing a major tilt in the global economy.

In the April of 2020 we had been researching the UK and the US Education sectors and we researched top Universities in both regions with a focus on the top 100. Looking at the findings in the UK first, we found that Universities including Oxford and London School of Economics (LSE) were maintaining Not Secure homepages which simply was totally illogical let alone non-compliant and in breach of UKDPA and GDPR. We wrote several times to each of the Universities in question informing them of their insecure and vulnerable position and yet again, our actionable intelligence and warnings were totally ignored. On 11 May, the British supercomputer Archer was breached. It was initially reported that the breach had been associated with Russian infiltration for Crypto mining, however it was not long after that the real reason for the breach of Archer was disclosed.

Archer is used by leading universities, researchers, pharmaceutical companies, and others within the medical profession to collate research data and in 2020 all Covid-19 research data. Universities like Oxford receive some £120 million annually for research and many others within their field would collate their research with Archer. As always, we researched Archer and there, as bold as anything, shockingly, the homepage was Not Secure with the digital certificate having expired in April 2020. The digital certificate had expired several weeks before Archer was breached. We continued researching and discovered other Archer-type supercomputers around Europe, all connected, had surprisingly been breached within the space of days. I am pleased to report that Oxford and some other Universities have finally listened, although it took months, or may have learnt the hard way, but had replaced their digital certificate providing them, finally, with Authentication, Encryption, and Data Integrity. I cannot say the same for Archer or the Edinburgh University where it is housed as both are Not Secure to this date www.archer.ac.uk www.epcc.ed.ac. uk (end of January 2021).

Towards the end of 2020, Cardiff University was awarded, for the second year in a row, the best Cybersecurity University to study and undertake a degree in cybersecurity. We had researched them as part of our earlier program on Universities however, decided to check again. Rather embarrassingly for the University, the award was great, however surely rather hollow as it was maintaining a Not Secure homepage. I personally know the Professor there and informed her of the issue. She confirmed PKI and certificates were not part of their curriculum or an area she was conversant with and that she would need to brush up on the area. Several weeks later it was secure again. It once again confirmed leading Universities as well as thousands of organisations have limited to no control or management of this critical security area.

In the US we undertook similar research. One of our leading research experts is a US citizen who now lives in the UK with his family. He is an ex-Military senior chap. He leads many of our US research programs with a passion that is rare and hard to find. I am truly indebted to him. He is unwavering and totally dedicated, he is unquestionably an incredible asset to the company. When he ran the US Education research program he was totally shocked at the outright systemic negligence, and that included the Ivy League Universities. I guess when we read about Clemson University receiving a $111 million grant to teach cybersecurity to the US manufacturing sector, we puzzled over what the hell they would be taught given the fact that we wrote to them several weeks beforehand warning them that their homepage was Not Secure and remains that way to this day (end of January 2021).

What has become abundantly clear is that our governments, our agencies, far too many so-called security experts, our healthcare, and our education systems, on both sides of the pond, have, and continue to let us down, through oversight, ignorance, or incompetence so far as good basic security goes. Many people within governments seemingly do not understand what Not Secure means along with the insecurity and implications. The agencies clearly have their own agenda, and love of all things TLS/SSL related, and far too many security experts ignore basic security measures especially internet facing security and PKI. Our Education sectors clearly do not understand or teach basic cybersecurity yet get awarded $billions collectively and handed awards for being great at teaching cyber... The fact is with the $billions being spent on cybersecurity, it is clearly not being maximised and certainly not well spent, in many cases it could be said that it is being squandered. The cyberwar we are in is raging and our leaders are not only acting like rabbits in the headlights, but they are also not taking steps to ensure basics are being addressed let alone managed properly. This is the single biggest reason we have seen cybercrime losses go from a few hundred $million to $trillions in the space of 20 years. I use the term regularly and it is one that the legal teams and executives need to consider more often and it this, was the cyberattack due to complacency or due to being complicit?

The recent breach of SolarWinds, a global leading cybersecurity, government's major player who has unquestionably all the bells and whistles in their armoury, thousands of staff, $billions in revenue, and in future contracts, and yet was breached due to not managing an internet facing domain and what is in fact, the unmanaged expiry of a single digital certificate.

Cybercriminals may have developed incredible malware, we know that, however SolarWinds was breached by a hijacked domain and then the adversaries stood up to www.avsvmcloud.com which ultimately gained them Digital Trust due to Domain Admin Access. Once that position was achieved, the attackers moved laterally and even took SolarWinds's digital certificates, laced them with their Malware (Sunburst), and distributed them to thousands of clients. Once again, the access point may be put down to a single missing digital certificate that made the initial domain hijacking possible. It is certainly not their only insecure domain or certificate issue, it is just the one that was used to enable infiltration. That oversight and missing certificate may end up costing, collectively more than $1 trillion. And yet our comprehensive research shows that all parties involved so far in this breach are still Not Secure facing and connected to the internet several weeks after the initial breach and that includes SolarWinds themselves.

12
NOT SECURE, THE VATICAN AND HEALTHCARE

Not Secure: What does it mean?

In 2016, Google Chrome decided they would try to address and assist the market and enable greatly improved security by enforcing better domain security. That included marking all Hypertext Transfer Protocol (HTTP) sites as 'Not Secure' from July 2018. It had been something Google, Mozilla, and other ISPs had been debating for several years as more and more protocols and breaches were occurring via weak internet security and more importantly, the domains connecting to the internet. Such vulnerabilities were constantly being exploited and no longer just to digitally eavesdrop. These vulnerabilities were easily exploitable. By doing so, this move would reduce vulnerabilities and increase security to the masses, a Planet Scale change. The move from HTTP to HTTPS but uses a Secure Socket Layer (SSL) that ensured encryption of the data that is passed from servers to browsers. In simple terms the different protocols make it possible for website servers to transfer data to a browser such as Chrome, one encrypted (HTTPS), and one not (HTTP). This enabled interaction with websites in a far safer and more secure manner and prevented man-in-the-middle attacks, authentication, data integrity, and encryption. When managed properly, it would vastly reduce digital ID theft and PII data theft. The only challenge was ensuring everyone adopted and migrated, and with some 2 billion domains, it would not prove to be an easy task to adopt the new HTTPS protocol.

A large percentage of people and organisations were so busy building new domains that the legacy domains were frequently overlooked, ignored, and neglected. This meant DANGER. This also meant they became, by default, insecure, and by doing so, also made them, unknowingly, easy targets due to the fact that the data was no longer encrypted but kept in plain text format as opposed to ciphertext.

DOI: 10.1201/9781003204145-12

84 STUXNET TO SUNBURST

Domain ecosystems typically pool and share data collection, not just for a business to enable data sharing and improved customer knowledge, but also for customer experience. No one wants to put their details in time after time, for example. Data harvesting is a huge, commercially driven area on its own, people's preferences, holidays, clothes, food types, cars, locations, and so on would all prove to have incredible value. In fact, the metric of numbers of peoples' PII data would be used to calculate the company's overall value for an IPO or similar. When companies learnt how to benefit from having numerous domains, and wider reach, they possibly overlooked the fact and maybe did not realise, that all connected domains had to be secure by also being updated to use HTTPS. In other words, like a chain is only as strong as its weakest link, so a company was only as secure as its weakest domain. A company that, for example has 50 domains requires all 50 to be using valid HTTPS protocols and valid digital certificates. If one is not, and they are connected, it can relegate the entire 50 to an insecure position.

We have just finished discussions with a major technology giant on this very issue after we discovered nearly two dozen of their domains that were Not Secure covering one country. Initially their Chief Security Advisor told me they were fake sites and when I pointed out these Not Secure domains linked directly into the mothership, they confirmed they were legacy. Strange then that all are live, Not Secure, and show today's date and time. Such a position leaves the organisation and all their clients totally vulnerable. I am sure the CSA is a very knowledgeable person and this week declared, with great enthusiasm, that they have hit $billions in security revenues, does little to confirm the woeful, negligent, and incompetence demonstrated by their oversights.

In simple terms, making all domains utilise HTTPS means everyone would benefit from the following:

1. Encryption – encrypting the exchanged data to keep it secure from eavesdroppers. That means that while the user is browsing a website, nobody can 'listen' to their conversations, track their activities across multiple pages, or steal their information.
2. Data integrity – data cannot be modified or corrupted during transfer, intentionally or otherwise, without being detected.

NOT SECURE, THE VATICAN AND HEALTHCARE   85

3. Authentication – proves that users communicate with the intended website. It protects against man-in-the-middle attacks and builds user trust, which translates into other business benefits.

This HTTPS milestone meant all domains required updating and was a great opportunity to update and address their domains security, the S part of HTTPS would be known as standing for Secure. Unfortunately, history will also show that this situation created one of the biggest waves of insecure digital front doors at organisations, governments, and companies. Of the circa 2 billion domains in the world today, there is a considerable percentage that remain Not Secure meaning the domain owner of the actual site cannot be authenticated, the data is not encrypted, and the data lacks integrity and can be easily and often readily manipulated. It also means visitors and users of domains had to be vigilant and we know that simply does not happen. In essence it became a cybercriminal's golden opportunity to identify, easily and readily, infiltrate and gain plain text data, and exfiltrate that they could then encrypt and demand Ransomware payment for. They could also hijack domains and take them over. This simple identification of vulnerable domains is the main reason we have witnessed a huge escalation of Ransomware over the last two years. Cybercriminals have gained easy access and not only exfiltrated data, but they have also encrypted the plain text and demanded ransom payments before providing (sometimes) the decryption keys to enable decryption. Ransomware over the last two years has grown in use to become one of the most notable cyberattacks, and there are many to choose from.

A sector that is literally plagued with Ransomware attacks due to being systemically insecure is the Healthcare sector. One example of this is the Union Hospital of New Jersey www.uhnj.org who was breached in August 2020. They were maintaining a Not Secure (unencrypted) domain, their homepage. Immediately once they received the Ransomware demands and closed computer systems, they consulted with the State and their Insurers. Their CEO Shereef Elnahal, the State, and the Insures decided to pay the $675k ransom payment to get back the hospital's highly sensitive patient PII and medical data. So, to explain this let me confirm. The data should have been encrypted but was not due to being Not Secure in the first place by having an obsolete and invalid digital certificate. The homepage on the address toolbar read, Not Secure. Cybercriminals gained access via this domain and then encrypted the plain text data using their own encryption key. In simple terms they took over command and control of the data. They then offered to sell the original owner of the data the encryption key to enable them to decrypt the data back to a form they could use. So the payment was made and the encrypted key was provided. That is basically how Ransomware works. Once the encryption key is received, it, hopefully, enables the data to be decrypted and then re-encrypted with an expensive lesson learnt. However, if the domain remains insecure, due to PKI/certificate misconfiguration or lack of a valid certificate being continually left and ignored, the data, still in plain text form can be read in plain text, exfiltrated, and re-encrypted again and again. Should a cyberattacker gain access through say a planted backdoor whilst they had C2. If this sounds like a revolving door, it very much is. Several emails and correspondence with Shereef, the CEO of UHNJ, and their domain remain Not Secure several months later. They are simply inviting the next breach. The first time was negligent, and this continued position must be considered criminal negligence.

In July last year (yes, it is 1 January 2021 as I type), the Vatican was subject to a major cyber breach. It was not their first, sadly, I suspect it will not be their last. However, this attack was quickly blamed as a Chinese State-sponsored attack. David Sanger of the *New York Times* wrote on 28 July 2020: 'Chinese hackers infiltrated the Vatican's computer networks over the past three months; a private monitoring group has concluded in an apparent espionage effort before beginning sensitive negotiations with Beijing.' The breach received international coverage and criticism. With over 1.3 billion followers, the PII data retained by the Vatican was extensive. On the actual day of the Vatican breach, we were alerted and, as always, ran Whitethorn Shield®. We always want to gain insight and get a baseline of internet facing and connected security as part of our efforts to understand criminal and more importantly, cybercriminal attacks. Within a short period of time, the team had pulled together a full initial audit of their 85 domains and subdomains which showed 82 out of the 85 domains were in fact being maintained with suboptimal internet facing security. In other words, 82 of the Vatican's domains were Not Secure

NOT SECURE, THE VATICAN AND HEALTHCARE 87

including their homepage www.vatican.va which it remains to this day, again inviting further attacks. Put simply, they had no defence and provided none for their followers.

The perfect storm had been created, and due to continued negligence, was left insecure after the breach. What made this particularly frustrating was that due to Covid-19 the only way the Vatican's followers could follow, interact, or donate to their Church was by doing so online. This meant the 1.3 billion followers could in fact become 1.3 billion victims of digital crimes, now and in the future. We contacted the Vatican, the UK Ambassador to the Vatican made calls and sent three emails over a period of three months. Finally, when we were interviewed and our research and findings were shared with the Catholic News Agency, who published a damning second article, which included our research and findings following the breach, the Vatican acknowledged our correspondence, but are still yet to address the issues…

Our research that typically follows the announcement of a breach, SolarWinds and FireEye are no exception, we spend considerable time researching internet facing positions. In a separate chapter I will cover in detail the SolarWinds's breach and the intelligence that has come to light in the last several days, and which continues to do so. Suffice to say, without exception, every breach we have researched, the company have had suboptimal internet facing positions with Not Secure domains rendering them, and their clients, highly vulnerable. As mentioned earlier, we are all connected by cables, electronic devices, servers, and the cloud. If a cybercriminal, thousands of miles away wants to breach a company, where do you think they start.

Open-source Intelligence (OSINT) is a totally legal, non-intrusive multi-method (qualitative and quantitative) for collecting, analysing, and making decisions about data which is accessible in publicly available sources that can be used for intelligence positioning. The intelligence community refers the term Open to overt, publicly available sources as opposed to clandestine or covert sources. OSINT has been around in one form or another for hundreds of years, however with the advent of instant communications and immediate information transfer, a vast amount of actionable and predictive intelligence can be obtained from public, unclassified sources.

There are many major internet facing OSINT providers and one could argue that cybercriminals should not be given access to them, however, that is a totally separate and different discussion. It does not take a rocket scientist to utilise the capability and as mentioned, of the 2 billion domains, a huge percentage are currently insecure and highly vulnerable. If you ask a corporate to introduce their head of internet security, chances are it will be a role that is not actually any single individual responsible for the area and given the fact many companies, like the Vatican have 85 domains and NASA has 23,699, you can start to appreciate it is not a quick click and check. Internet security should be one of the single largest area of management and concern. It must have total control and management daily, however as breaches clearly and continually demonstrate, including governments, it is often an afterthought and often not considered at all until something goes woefully wrong, and even then, can still be ignored as above. It is a major reason for initial infiltration and breaches. The malware and code may be sophisticated, and gaining access is typically the digital equivalent of keys being left in a car or a front door open on a house.

In August 2020, I wrote an article for a well-known, globally acknowledged industry leading publication in the specialist field of Digital Forensics. The article was on Cryptography and the modern Enigma of digital certificates. The article was being featured and with a readership of many of the leaders in the security field across the UK and Europe, the distribution list alone would be something of a coup to harvest and exploit. When the article was published, I wanted to share it on social media (mainly LinkedIn with nearly 30,000 followers), and to share our insights, it can of course be a powerful platform. When I went to link the online version, there right in front of me was a Not Secure homepage. There was no way I could link this page, it was as bad as the UK government's Computer misuse Act (CMA), the UK Quantum Group, or a Hiscox having Not Secure homepages, which although unbelievable, all had until we alerted them. It is said that many people relish learning, however it is much harder to find someone who wants to be taught without their request.

Taking a considerate and sympathetic approach, I informed the owner of the Digital Forensic publication, someone who seemingly holds me in high respect. However, what ensued was little short of an all-out argument and a barrage of denial. There was a several thousand-word, six-page article I had spent considerable time writing and

NOT SECURE, THE VATICAN AND HEALTHCARE 89

being made available online via a Not Secure and Industry domain. As calmly as I could, I shared our OSINT research and findings which we had undertaken. The publication owner was adamant they had a valid certificate and the certificate matched the domain. One by one we ran through our findings and finally, found that one third-party supplier, who supplied some of the creative backdrops and pictures had supplied these in HTTP. The domain was in fact being relegated to the least secure content being used. It was immediately addressed and bingo, a beautiful Secure domain, that we were delighted to share. The owner has over 30 years of Industry leading experience and was effectively bamboozled by a third party supplying insecure code and could not work out why, possibly even more concerning, the website was being published and not a single person raised the issue or addressed it and every one of its thousands of readers are in the field of security.

Interestingly, a government, that will remain undisclosed, was breached last summer across several of their major operations including their treasury. We quickly sprang into action and assisted them in a similar way. They were maintaining Not Secure domains and upon research and investigation, we later showed it to be the initial infiltration point. They thought their domains were secure, however made incorrect assumptions. When we provided our intelligence, we showed their third-party supplier who produced the code for their National flag that was being used on every one in their site, was making them insecure. Considering further developments, including Class Action cases, the responsibility and liability for ensuring security will be an interesting area to watch and that will include shareholders holding Boards to account. As a footnote, no website should ever be published without security checks being made, at publication and ongoing. Another shocking example is by one of the Queen's direct descendants. They have set up a Covid-19 testing company in 2020 for immediately collecting PII data and from the word go are breaching GDPR regulations by maintaining Not Secure websites. These are immediately open to attack, as are their client's and their PII data, since their launch in 2020. Clearly no one is checking before publishing websites let alone maintaining them.

Without wishing to seemingly be too pedantic, it must be every company's responsibility to ensure that when they publish new domains and launch them, they are fully tested prior to going live, this simply is not the case and should be a prerequisite. Cigarettes all over the world carry a Health Warning message, can you imagine if that was not the case, and some did and some didn't? Someone contracting a respiratory condition could say the supplier did not warn them. Equally, it is a company's responsibility to ensure that correct controls and management of all their internet facing domains are secure, not just a few. By addressing this one issue, we would see a great improvement of and secure positions and a great reduction of successful cyberattacks. People are simply leaving their keys in their car or in the front door, in a high crime area and expecting nothing to happen. It is nothing short of negligence and due to cybercriminals having OSINT capabilities and actually using AI to alert them of Not Secure domains due to certificate invalidity, mismatching domains and certificates, they identify their targets and launch their attacks as our research continually shows.

In the early winter of 2020, we designed and developed Whitethorn Shield® as an extension to Whitethorn® to provide proactive, managed services to organisations that wanted to maximise their internet presence and footprint but without compromising their security. However, by their current oversight, negligence and focus elsewhere, they were exposing the company to more harm and attacks. Their businesses are totally exposed and highly vulnerable as are their visitors and clients because of their own negligence. This one factor is fuelling the incredible losses more than any other in the world today. It is not the sheer sophistication of a Stuxnet or Sunburst attack, it is the ease of which access can, and is being obtained and next to nothing is being done about it. As of 5 January 2021, the NSA have finally taken on board our constant dialogue and produced their version and paper of Whitethorn Shield® in the form of an Information Sheet titled 'Eliminating obsolete TLS Protocol Configurations.' This is a major milestone which we are delighted with, however, as I said to a Nuclear Energy company with millions of clients, the acknowledgement is one thing, without action, it is little more than lip service. I must follow the Nuclear Energy Company as several weeks has passed since I provided evidence of their insecure position and not heard anything back; clearly security is high on their agenda.

13
AUSTRALIA'S FRUSTRATION WITH CHINA AND ASSISTING THE FBI

In an interview on 19 June 2020, Australia's Prime Minister Scott Morrison said that the government and Australian institutions were constantly suffering cyberattacks and being targeted by ongoing, what was being called, sophisticated state-based type cyber hacks. Mr Morrison said the cyberattacks were widespread, covering 'all levels of government' as well as essential services and businesses. He declined to identify a specific state actor and said no major personal data breaches had been made. The attacks have happened over many months and are increasing, he said. The Prime Minister went on to say his announcement was intended to raise public awareness and to urge businesses to improve their defences. But he stressed that 'malicious' activity was also being seen globally, making it not unique to Australia. We decided to research numerous Australian government departments and Australian companies to gain insight on these statements.

As part of our ongoing research around the world and the fact we have been working with colleagues, friends, and associates in the industry in Australia, we researched further and over several weeks found very concerning and systemic issues which again, were certainly not unique to Australia, they were a major concern especially at government level. As Scott Morrison had said, such malicious activity was not confined to Australia, however nor was the security incompetence and negligence that we also found. I wrote to the Prime Minister and several of those in the Parliament more than once as our research quickly showed a woeful trail of insecure organisations that demonstrated a total lack of internet facing and connected security. These findings, for example included Tony Abbott, the former Prime Minister whose own homepage for several months, www.tonyabbott. com.au, had been Not Secure and open to attacks and abuse.

DOI: 10.1201/9781003204145-13

In September 2020, it was announced that Service NSW, a major technical provider, had been breached with the data of 186,000 customers and staff being leaked, it was also confirmed that emails had also been compromised. The investigation showed that nearly 4 million documents were analysed to determine the severity of the breach including the theft of PII data. There was apparently no evidence of the MyServiceNSW data or the Service NSW databases being compromised. The attack was put down to a criminal attack and cyberattacks 'happen daily' was a comment made by a representative of Service NSW.

Our research was in full swing during the summer and our findings were, as mentioned, deeply concerning to say the least. I wrote again to the Prime Minister, Scott Morrison, Tony Abbott the previous Prime Minister, and Victor Domenillo the NSW Minister. Victor kindly replied to me and introduced me to a senior Service NSW employee, both Scott Morrision and Tony Abbott did not reply. That was quite strange as the MOs for cybercriminals were increasingly being shown as they were looking for insecure domains to launch attacks on and I had emailed, via Mr Abbott's own personal website, informing him that it was insecure and had been since the beginning of the year. It remains the same today, 2 January 2021.

The Person at NSW requested further information and at the same time I was contacted by the Australian Signals and Defence team and introduced to their head of cyber defence. A call was set up after email exchanges and I was asked to share some of our research and findings. In a call that lasted an hour, my early morning and Australia's late afternoon, an open conversation and disclosure of Tony Abbott's Not Secure website along with numerous others were shared with the two top Australian Cyber Defence chaps, whose names will remain anonymous. One was quite quiet, and the other led from the Australian Defence side. Throughout the conversation I was keen to put across, and share our research and findings, not just in Australia, but on a much wider geography, to which of course, they were in total agreement with. I covered our findings at Service NSW following their recent breach disclosure and our concerns of their plethora of insecure domains (still the same today) and the correlation between insecure internet facing and being targeted, then attacked. This was long before the SolarWinds breach and Domain Admin Access. There was not a single push back on the OSINT research or the findings and even a comment 'We know companies and organisations are leaving themselves wide open, we do not have the power to regulate or enforce, they make themselves secure or they don't,' interestingly the NCSC here in the UK have said similar things in correspondence with me and confirmed they have tried to alert people for three years or so of the dangers of obsolete TLS/SSL certificates ensuring security on domains. At the time, it seemed a reasonable statement, however upon reflection, it was quite hollow and simply does not help anyone, certainly not the Australian government, Australian organisations and people that are being constantly attacked due to their own, but possibly misunderstood position. I have kept in contact with the head of Cyber defence in Australia however, I suspect as part of Five Eyes, they too might have their own agenda, and their use of TLS and SSL certificates as part of their ongoing Computer Network Exploitation was, and is, widespread across all Cyber Defence Agencies as mentioned earlier in this book.

Australia, and more latterly, Scott Morrison has gone on record as declaring China as the outright culprit and declaring a position that will no longer tolerate the ongoing attacks. International relations between the two, although geographically close countries, has become strained, and a tit for tat trade war position adopted with vast increases on imports to prevent some trade, at the time of writing, mainly coal and wine. The part that Mr Morrison, Victor Domenillo, the NSW team are unequivocally overlooking is that as a Nation, they have simply dropped their guard in a near identical manner to the US and UK governments. They quite possibly never actually raised it so far as their connectivity to the internet goes, and due to being continuously insecure, have made the country insecure and an easy target. Their ongoing breaches are unquestionably occurring because of it. Cyberattackers will always select the path of least resistance and what better way to do so by being allowed easy access to a company's, or in this case, a country's computer systems and data. As I write, we also checked several of the key domains we flagged including the several Service NSW and Tony Abbott's homepage and all remain insecure. Maybe news of the SolarWinds breach and use of insecure domains and certificates has not reached there yet.

Whilst some of the teams were researching Australia and their security posture, we decided to undertake research across the US in

50 States. The 2020 election was looming and our earlier findings on Alaska's insecure position concerned me. To reiterate, we undertook OSINT research on Alaska (I known Alabama is the first) and the findings were simply unbelievable. Not secure homepage for over a year, 29 CVE, many highly rated, some critical and dating back to 2013 and this site captured all PII of Alaskan constituents, you could also register to vote in the forthcoming elections. Alaska State had also suffered a cyberattack in 2019. The initial report was dated 29 May 2020. The Research continued alphabetically and encompassed the actual voting including centralised voting.

Through one of our partners, we were introduced to the FBI given the findings at Alaska and started a dialogue with them. Not too different to the conversations we had later with the Australian Defence team in as much that the research and findings were taken on board, however the FBI declared each State's internet security was not their focus. We had written both directly to Alaska and indirectly via a good friend who knew the team responsible for security to inform (by now to also alert) them of their position. No action was taken, and Alaska remained Not Secure, despite generous government monies and funds being made available to ensure secure States and systems in the run up to the election. Clearly this bolstered the State coffers but did not improve any security.

During the summer of 2020, our research and the findings made for ever increasing and concerning insights. It was at the point of discovering a Korean DNS within the US Vote.gov system that we had a further conversation directly with the US FBI team. The DNS server, one of only four DNS, had the ability to infiltrate and exfiltrate as much data directly to a Korean University as it wanted and no one even knew about it. Someone had gained access and inserted, by manipulating the Vote.gov system a Korean DNS. I am sure I have no need to explain how 300 million US citizens' data and details could be captured, manipulated, and abused, however there it was as large as life and we had identified it. The FBI did I seem to recall say thank you, however, our research on the back of the Westech International and their Maze Ransomware breach was also not of interest unless it, along with all our other research, was provided for free of charge. We appreciate everyone is busy and things can be missed; however, the entire Intelligence community on the year of the election and only

AUSTRALIA BATTLES WITH CHINA

months prior to the election date were unaware of a Korean placed DNS within the US central voting system and we were working for free to assist. Surely that balance cannot be okay.

The Korean DNS was successfully shut down by the FBI, and I cannot confirm how long it had been active. We carried on with our research and decided at that point to go all out and research all 50 US States and build a full, comprehensive report. State by State our research showed a systemic lack of internet facing security, and although was by no means exhaustive, it certainly was comprehensive. Do not forget a cybercriminal only needs one single access point and we were finding dozens upon dozens, sometimes within a single State. Not Secure homepages, old CVE's dating back a decade plus and many critical. We knew from trying to contact Alaska we could not afford the time trying to contact every State and alert them and besides, very worryingly, it had proven very time consuming and fruitless to even try. The report took several weeks, and it showed the weakest areas and areas of major concern: outdated software and software patching, insecurity facing the internet, unmanaged, uncontrolled subdomains with invalid certificates and so on. Our US head of research became more than a tad concerned to the point of being almost in shock at just how bad it was. I am not using the term subjectively here; it was a cybercriminal's playground, and no one seemed to care about it. It was around the same time the CIA and NSA took lots of flak for spending all their budgets on building offensive cyber capability and at the cost of and ignoring defence. Our research and findings confirmed this in abundance. As part of our report, we produced a heat map, green for good, yellow for not good, and red for major vulnerabilities and risks. Not one State is green, many are bright yellow, and far too many are a bright crimson red with Delaware being the worst, still what damage can Delaware's insecure State and government ever do to the US commerce and economy.

Alaska State suffered a further cyberattack and data breach in early October 2020 and strangely enough, the Alaska domain was given a brand new certificate making it now secure for the first time in many months. I cannot comment on why the new certificate was placed on the Alaska domain two weeks after being breached and backdated to pre the breach. Alaska also suffered a breach in January 2019 when over 100,000 households that applied for public assistance were breached and that attack was blamed on Russian infiltration. Is it me or does there seem to be a clear pattern that looks and feels like continued negligence and poor leadership? It is clear no one is learning which is rather bizarre and incredibly concerning. A common comment from US experts confirms that 'defences at home are wildly insufficient' and such comments are not wrong, but what is being done to improve it apart from throwing $billions and wasting it on buzzword creations and pretend security?

Once the data was collated on the 50 US States, we extended it to include several Senators' and the US Presidents' websites too. We found a dozen Senators maintaining insecure domains, which could be easily attacked, and several of the US Presidents' domains were also insecure. We informed all parties via our US-based and well-connected third party. Many of the Senators' domains were quite quickly addressed. The Donald Trump sites were to a great extent, however several were not including www.aws.donaldjtrump.com which remained Not Secure up to, and post being breached also in October 2020 and as my other screen shows as I type, is not secure today due to a lack of a digital certificate. We researched further using OSINT technology and capability and discovered numerous connected domains that were also insecure and that included US government domains and the even the White House. These positions remain Not Secure as I type several months after being alerted. www.email.whitehouse.com.

To confirm, OSINT technology is using publicly available information and data, it does not go beyond anything other than what is facing the internet from a firewall outward. Think of it as looking through a window without ever entering inside the building. The difference between using OSINT ethically and using OSINT for nefarious purposes is a simple distinction. Ethical use of OSINT stops at the front door whereas a cybercriminal will use the same intelligence to simply storm in, or in the case of many, just stroll right in. Of the two billion domains in existence, or thereabouts, the size and scale of the problem is vast. The government seemingly do not want to address it, possibly because of the sheer scale, and besides, the misunderstanding and vulnerability has served them very well to date and continues to do so. Companies over the last decade have been remiss, overlooked, or simply been negligent and that includes many governments. At the time

AUSTRALIA BATTLES WITH CHINA

of writing, our research shows several DOD, MOD, and Defence domains totally insecure facing and connected to the internet which is nothing short of utter madness. I mentioned the missile company that has been insecure since 2013 and building missiles for their government and they have ignored several emails to date yet undoubtedly could suffer an attack to gain access to the US government, if not have already www.marvingroup.com.

There has been an inordinate amount of blaming the Russians, the Chinese, the Koreans, and some will undoubtedly be valid, however, surely a question of who started this and why, and after starting it, why did everyone drop their guard and use it as an excuse to become negligent across the entire country and globe? Can laying blame stop the haemorrhaging and losses, of course not. What is required is a total focus on perimeter defences and that means internet facing security. Just unplug everything and stop using computers and you will unquestionably be much safer. Over the last 12 months we have witnessed more breaches than ever before and at the same time, seen more online trading than ever before. The correlation of Covid-19, working from home, and increased losses is no coincidence. If you connect you are vulnerable, if you are not secure you will be infiltrated, this time it is not by those wanting to get to know you better for analytical purposes, it will be to enact criminal actions against you and that will never stop until internet security and PKI is prioritised, and not, at best, left to chance or an afterthought.

14

BLACKBAUD AND THIRD-PARTY TRUST

Blackbaud is a cloud provider that serves charities, socially good, not for profits, education, healthcare and religious organisations, and other sectors. Blackbaud is an American company that was founded by Anthony Bakker in New York in 1981. Their flagship product is a fundraising SQL database software, Raisers Edge. Their list of products continued being developed as they expanded into different lines and geographic areas. In 2019, Blackbaud announced it had over 45,000 clients and achieved record revenues for the year of $930 million plus and had over 3,500 staff.

Due to the extensive and extensive clientele within the specific sectors, Blackbaud had something of a monopoly and clients made assumptions that if Blackbaud's services were good enough for Charity A, then they should also outsource their business and administration to them. Sadly, much of this was done without too many checks or thorough due diligence and Blackbaud clearly became, like far too many organisations, complacent and ignored their own security, which in turn due to the company's connectivity, undermined their client's security. No one knew, and no one would find out until the inevitable day when Blackbaud was breached, and the consequential breaches started being felt.

In May 2020, Blackbaud was breached and the attackers managed to exfiltrate PII data and corporate data from hundreds, possibly thousands of their clients before being detected. The breach was made public in July 2020 several weeks later. This should have acted as a wake-up call for those winning outsourced technical deals and those outsourcing. However, what has become apparent on this, and many more breaches, including Westech International and other DOD and DHS suppliers, utility companies, governments, health companies, and even as in this case, charities and not for profit organisations,

DOI: 10.1201/9781003204145-14

99

is that no one is undertaking proper due diligence on their providers, suppliers, or clients. Assumptions are simply being made. Is it too much to consider that just as in the game of chess, a pawn or two, may be sacrificed to achieve the taking of a queen? In the same way, a subcontractor or an outsourcing smaller company may not be the real target, but a route to entry. You bet and if, as in the case of ongoing security negligence at Blackbaud, the fact they had hundreds of similar clients that were guilty of not undertaking any due diligence and were not addressing their own security, they too would also fall victim.

In the world of training and personal development, it is acknowledged that ideally you want to say less to more people. The same stance can be seen by virtue of social media or the internet and domains. The multiple use of the same message to thousands, even millions is perfect. Perversely, the same situation applies in reverse for cybercriminals, why attack a single company if you can get to hundreds, even thousands?

The Blackbaud breach followed the trend of the company being infiltrated, yes you guessed it, whilst they had numerous insecure and unmanaged domains, and then were infiltrated totally unbeknown and malware injected. At the same time, the fashion continued to not only encrypt some of the data but also to remove some to leverage their position. One can never assume a criminal will have integrity, they are a criminal after all, and may always sell on data, or even return like a farmer reaping their crop annually to increase their yield, there is nothing better than annual or repeat business.

We undertook research on Blackbaud's internet facing position just days after their breach and are convinced we would find a plethora of systemic insecure domains, subdomains that would be easily identified pre the breach by cyberattackers, we were not surprised to find our suspicions confirmed. The trend was unquestionable and the correlation evident. It was almost as if some of these huge technical giants wanted to either call it on, or could they collectively be so negligent? I have this morning researched and there, as bold as can be, are numerous Blackbaud Not Secure domains, invalid, expired, non-matched certificates, and so on, this must be considered and seen as criminal negligence and treated as such. Security is not about Blackbaud or any company that gets breached, moreover it should be the fact the company has ignored and placed their clients in high-risk position and then to be breached due to their incompetence and neglect.

BLACKBAUD AND THIRD-PARTY TRUST   101

The question that is simply not being posed by outsourced providers or outsourcing clients is what is our ongoing internet security posture like, will outsourcing strengthen our security position or greatly reduce it? This should be mandatory during the outsourcing discussions and just like buying Cyber Insurance, undertaking any M&A on corporate activities, be evidenced. Without being discourteous to any security professional or CISO, very few can evidence what their own internet facing security looks like and none their internal PKI and that, as the conclusion of the hundreds of companies and breached companies confirms. How can tech giants have entire countries for several years out of date certificates and Not Secure homepages linked directly to the Mothership and not expect security issues and liabilities due to such negligence?

A fact very few people know, even security experts must guess at is the fact a new, Gold Standard laptop, typically has around 250,000 certificates on it with typically over 20,000 unique certificates on it. That includes root certs, TLS, and SSL which are preloaded for software, links, etc. When a company, government, or Education facility takes delivery of thousands of new laptops or equipment (typically made in Asia), who has their equipment scanned? Who knows what is on each device and if there is a plant or two returning all data to a Mothership and ready to take over C2 upon a simple command? I have never received an answer to this question, however why does Microsoft issue software updates complete with Chinese Internet Network Information Centre (CNNIC) certificates to everyone apart for the DHS, for example? Google blacklisted all CNNIC certificates after they were found to being used for misusing them for domain access in 2015. CNNIC is a Chinese State-owned Certificate Authority who manage the entire CN domains. In that same year, Google, Mozilla, and Microsoft responded to a misused CNNIC certificate by the Egyptian company MCS Holdings which was found to have made it possible to impersonate Google domains and intercept the data flow. Only this week Google announced that as of April they would no longer accept and remove the Spanish Certificate Authority Camerfirma due to irregularities. On the face of it, that is a nuisance for Camerfirma, however the implications are much wider as every client and customer's domains using a TLS certificate issued by Camerfirma will, as of April, become Not Secure and therefore, if those clients do not address replacements of said certificates will potentially be open to attacks of domain hijacking and take over including man-in-the-middle attacks and denial of service.

In an update from Google on the CNNIC they said: 'Following an investigation and the disclosure of bogus certificates, the company have decided that CNNIC root and EV CA will no longer be recognised in Google products.' While Google and CNNIC believed that no further unauthorised digital certificates had been issued, and that misused certificates were outside of MCS holdings test network, CNNIC would be working to prevent any future incidents. The lesson to learn from all of this, even the tech giants get spoofed by digital certificates, Shadow websites, and are caught out. CNNIC certificates within any enterprise is a risky business and one that there are many, many options on. Why Microsoft still issue CNNIC certificates to everyone except the DHS is undoubtedly questionable.

We cover CAs in another chapter and how all CAs have had a history or catastrophic issuance of incorrect and compromised certificates, they are also often challenged to identify and revoke certificates, upgrade them as required and so on. Make no mistake, when a root certificate is compromised, so can the entire enterprise be and this, along with millions of unknown certificates internally making up a company's PKI let alone those providing, or not, security facing the internet, are typically unknown, uncontrolled, and unmanaged. Industry estimates suggest some 1.5% of certificates are rogue, compromised, or prove to cause a security issue. That was before Whitethorn® and is very subjective. We believe it is possibly as high as 5% plus, and most organisations have at least twice the number of actual certificates than their wildest guess, it is certainly a big number.

Let us take a single, Gold Standard laptop, for example. With 250,000 certificates, 20,000 being unique certificates, if we lay over the numbers $20,000 \times 1.5\% = 300$, if you use our guide of circa 5% it is 1,000 certificates and remember, it only takes one. In last year's extended meeting with a global cybersecurity firm with hundreds of thousands of staff, their new Gold Standard laptop, along with the Head of Country and PKI team. Whitethorn® showed 287,000 certificate instances and over 30,000 unique certificates. The usual plethora of expired, weak cipher, and deprecated certificates were in there but why might there be, totally unbeknown to them, seven CNNIC certificates with 999 years validity, and what can only be described as having the ability of full administration rights with the ability to take command and control? Initially their PKI team was in total shock and wanted to pull their engineering team over the coals. Several months later they pushed back and said, they had a small Chinese presence, so it was okay. We all knew it was utter nonsense and 999 years for any certificate is simply unprecedented let alone incredibly dangerous. It gave the ability to switch, as and when desired, C2 on the company and their thousands of clients including government. It had nothing at all to do with security for them or their clients.

Assumptions are made and that is of course human nature, however what we have here is from company's making assumptions on their own security, outsource providers assuming they, and their client are secure, DNS and CDN providers making assumptions up and down the supply chain with hundreds of Ports open, CAs not managing certificates correctly, Cloud providers making assumptions to the DNS, CDN, outsource providers and ultimately the clients and we have assumptions literally coming out of our ears. The truth be told, not one, not even one of these entities can, with any assurance or confidence, confirm security facing the internet or their PKI and it seems as if everyone is okay with this.

Blackbaud's consequential breach tally is currently more than 125 companies including charities and counting. The breach seems to be yesterday's news and the new norm. This breach, as thousands of others, was due to their initial negligence. SolarWinds breach, which will potentially affect tens of thousands, was due to similar oversight and negligence. It has been over ten years since Olympic Games and Stuxnet, the world's first digital weapon which misused digital certificates, and last month's SolarWinds breach shows more than a passing resemblance of that attack. The breach replicated a near carbon copy by virtue of the certificates being laced with malware. The desired game plan may have been somewhat different; however, the destruction and disruption will be similar, but on a much bigger scale let alone the fact this attack was by our adversaries and will affect millions of people. Sad to say that upon researching as of writing, SolarWinds and FireEye still both have suboptimal and not secure positions facing the internet.

15
STUXNET TO SUNBURST

'There are risks and costs to action. But they are far less that the long-term risks of comfortable inaction' John F. Kennedy.

Lessons can, and are typically unquestionably invaluable, however every scholar must be receptive to being taught. In 2010 the world's first digital weapon, Stuxnet, set a new benchmark for cyberwarfare, it also set a new tone of just what could be achieved and covertly, through digital manipulation. Following the disclosure of Stuxnet, the world's superpowers watched on as Stuxnet was forensically dissected and as the findings and revelations surface, they almost, although silently declared, if it is good enough for the US, it is good enough for us. 2010 will go down as the year cyberwar came of age and Stuxnet would be its father. There is some conjecture around the timing and origination between Flame and Duqu, however, whichever was first, it was not the headline, Stuxnet could not and would not be toppled as the world's first digit weapon.

In 2013, the US cyberwar fighters were focused on the physical effects of Stuxnet and its collateral damage capabilities. How, from the lessons learned on Project Aurora and then Stuxnet, such lessons could serve them to be the dominant force in the cyberspace just as they had achieved within the Nuclear space. Cyberwar and the cyber breaches including infiltration and collection of data would prove to be slightly different and with a different cost of entry. Russia, China, and others treated cyber differently and played a much longer, and ultimately as we sit today, possibly a smarter game. They dealt with cyber congruently, as a set of collectives and utilised all its facets to their distinct advantage. Some would even go so far to say that whilst the US was puffing up their chests, almost looking for a fight, and have to date been found guilty of doing just that by their own government, China, Russia, and others were learning and being taught, and happy to be students.

DOI: 10.1201/9781003204145-15

In 2015, Russia had further developed and clearly honed their capability and moved from being the student, to fully graduating. They had carefully taken their education seriously and had learned well. They decided that Ukraine would be their inaugural, major target, and testing ground for their newly perfected digital capability. Russia, up until this point, had been sending in their 'Little Green Men' to cause chaos that disrupted the government. The Ukrainian power grid was widely known to be old, outdated, and somewhat antiquated. Some of it was so old in fact that it did not even use computers. On 23 December 2015, a cyberattack was launched against the Ukrainian power grid and is now widely accepted as the world's first ever attack on a power grid. Over 30 Ukraine substations were effectively switched off and nearly a quarter of a million people had no power for several hours, it could have been worse. The exercise is widely considered to have been a postulated attack by Russia as a warning. To demonstrate their capability, expose Ukraine vulnerabilities and to enforce compliance. It was very much a lesson on a large and potentially frightening scale.

Russia had developed new malware, or amended malware bought and readily available on the Dark Web that would become known as BlackEnergy. BlackEnergy was deployed into the Ukrainian systems by a phishing campaign across numerous corporate networks, in truth finding an access point in a country with very limited capability was always going to be easy. By achieving infiltration, they were able to take over Supervisory and Data Control Acquisition (SCADA) and simply, switch it off by taking over command and control (C2). As part of the attack, they disabled and effectively destroyed IT infrastructure components, caused the destruction of files stored on servers and workstations with KillDisk malware. At the same time and seemingly to demonstrate further disruption, they caused a Denial-of-Service attack on the grid's central call centre during the attack. As mentioned, Russia was already in a conflict with Ukraine and had been for some time, however this attack was silent, devastating, and used numerous lessons learned from Stuxnet five years earlier. It was an incredibly effective, stealth attack, and without a single tank being deployed or a shot fired. This attack is considered one of the first ventures by Russia into full blown cyberattacks and in truth, they seemed pretty good at it albeit their target had not adopted cutting-edge technology.

STUXNET TO SUNBURST

107

This attack would become known as Sandworm. Andy Ozment, of Homeland Security, went on to say, 'Although the Sandworm attack was not particularly sophisticated, it was incredibly effective. The two are not dependent upon one another.' As the intelligence was shared in Washington, internal research confirmed that BlackEnergy malware had been discovered across the US power grid. The effectiveness of a cyberattack is not dependent upon its level of sophistication. Often, it is more dependent upon the target's ability to defend themselves from such an attack and infiltration in the first place. Sadly, the lack of defence is typical and successful attacks are far too easy.

Sandworm and its presence were indeed a wake-up call for the US and its potential and capability to take over equipment on the grid including opening switches and circuits (Project Aurora) on demand, and even without an internet connection, could be catastrophic. It was, as David Sanger termed in his excellent book, *The Perfect Weapon*, the equivalent to a self-guiding missile.

A short while after the Ukrainian 'test run,' Russia focused their attention to cyberattacks in the US armed with freshly honed capability and irrefutable success. The target on this occasion would be the Democratic National Committee (DNC) and took place later in 2015 through to 2016. On 9 December, the CIA informed US legislators Intelligence community that Russia had conducted cyber-attacks and operations during the 2016 elections to assist Donald Trump in winning the presidency. Numerous agencies and private cybersecurity firms, including FireEye, concluded specifics tied Cozy Bear/Fancy Bear, who are known as Russian cyber force groups, had undertaken the attacks. The intelligence agencies also concluded that the Republican National Committee (RNC) as well as the DNC had been breached, however the intelligence gathered that the RNC was not leaked whereas the DNC was…

In April 2016, it was discovered that the Fancy Bear attacks were present within the DNC. The collating and analysis of all communications had been undertaken along with the theft of data. These attacks were part of a wider assault on US government departments and went undetected for months, possibly more than a year. It must have been incredibly difficult and strained when President Obama and President Vladimir Putin met at the G20 summit to discuss computer security issues in China in September 2016. In a joint statement

108 STUXNET TO SUNBURST

on 7 October 2016, the US department of Homeland Security and the office of the Director for National Intelligence stated that the US intelligence community was confident that the Russian government directed the breaches and the release of the obtained, or allegedly obtained material to interfere with the US election process.

The DNC, like far too many organisations, including governments, was still working as if it is all roses and pleasantries. It was not as they later found out. In the late summer of 2015, the US government was put on alert of the prospect of Russian attacks and when Special Agent Adrian Hawkins contacted the DNC, one of many failed attempts to do so and raise the alarm, but possibly one of the most prominent organisations in the year preceding elections, they may be attacked by Russia. In September he requested to speak to their security team, he eventually was put through to a contractor called Yared Tamene who was on contract as a generalist technical support guy and knew little about security. This was not part of his contract and he considered the call as much a spoof call more than anything serious. The two spoke again in November, several weeks later after Hawkins had left several, unreturned voicemails. It was mentioned at this time the infiltration and the 'calling home' nature implied it may be State sponsored. The FBI could see the data flowing out of the building, however, did not have the responsibility to protect privately owned computer networks. The challenge FBI Special Agent Hawkins encountered was a near identical situation that we had experienced with the Australian Defence (and many more) when they confirmed, and agreed with our findings, but could not enforce or drive changes to privately held companies. I find the situation with the ex-Prime Minister's insecure home page a tad more concerning that after months that has been ignored and left, unremedied, something must change.

Finally, in March 2016, Special Agent Adrian Hawkins and his team met with the DNC, a full six months following the initial alarm call. Much damage had been done and a whole heap of data had been stolen. Who would know how far it would go was a guessing game? During this period, it was well known that much of the US's political, government, and utilities had been infiltrated. It was systemic and Washington did not have all the answers, but with as much as 80% of all cyberattacks being launched against the US, inaction could no longer be an option. The US had been instrumental in developing cyberwar capability, and the same could not be said of their capability to defend against it. Considering the Hawkins DNC meeting, why did no one from the offices take a taxi or drive the half mile to the DNC offices for six months or escalate the information appropriately? In the security world, six minutes can be a lifetime and allow all manner of infiltration and yet here, on the year of election, people were too busy, too lacking in security knowledge to action what was right in front of them. There is a massive, serious lesson here as I can totally identify with and maybe it is because too many people cry wolf, we certainly need something to deal with this. When I inform the CEO of a mobile phone company or the CEO of a chemical company or indeed the board of Critical National Infrastructure of their insecure position, along with evidence, often, it is ignored, and interestingly, I sent this kind of message to all of these and many more including DOD and MOD both here and abroad regularly, and no replies. Many remain insecure and very few remediate, they just seemingly wait to be breached. Are people really that busy? It becomes interesting to see how many are breached later and just as Special Agent Hawkins struggled to get the DNC to listen and take action as a Federal Agent, we are equally challenged to inform, alert, and warn companies of their insecure position, this must change as the losses increase and the economy continues in a downward spiral. I have been trying to inform Microsoft for weeks of a major, country wide security issue, it seems people are simply too busy or too lacking in knowledge.

In the spring of 2016, Robert Hannigan launched a scathing attack against Silicon Valley's tech giants. Mr Hannigan had been the head of GCHQ UK for a year and a half, and his remit was to upgrade and bring GCHQ into the 21st century. In the *Financial Times* he was quoted as saying, 'Silicon Valley giants, no matter how much they dislike it, have become the Command-and-Control networks of choice for terrorists and criminals. This is an interesting comment and can be considered more than just a little hypocritical. Even though Mr Hannigan had a point, such capability and the weaponising of the internet originated and was very much due to the agencies' making. In conversations with Google, we asked the questions, how can in one minute they host a playcentre or primary school's home page, and in the next a paedophile home page and ring, or a terrorist group and the next home page for your local store? There seems to be little to no controls or assurance of the content that was being made available and hosted. It was earlier in 2020 that we offered to assist the FBI when we uncovered the entire trail of the Maze Ransomware organisations, names, IP addresses, contact details, and so on. It seemed rather bizarre then that the same Ransomware gang was using the same CDN, Cloudflare as the FBI was and the same CDN was providing digital certificates to the Ransomware group, based in China via their DNS. This, on the surface legitimised them, at least their domain.

We hypothesised that it would be far greater to ensure social responsibility for Google to assure all domains were socially acceptable and authentic and not being used for nefarious purposes. With cyberattacks causing losses into $trillions annually, was it right that Google, DNS, and CDNs should simply take the cash and not worry who they were hosting, facilitating, and enabling. In addition, knowing that when domains become Not Secure by virtue of Google and others HTTPS initiative, did they not have a moral duty? This thought, along with a commercial view, to assist organisations that were remiss and fell into the trap only to then be targeted, attacked, and breached could be managed as a service or solution. This conversation is still ongoing and one that I believe would make the world much safer and undoubtedly more secure. A proactive position rather than a reactive one could turn the tide and for once, in our favour.

As an organisation, we understand and empathise that security, expiring certificates, and becoming insecure may not be a company's mainstay focus. We also appreciate that many people may not have signed up for security as part of their daily remit, however, ultimately it may make the difference between thriving and surviving. Even the tech giants have had their ups and downs and with Ransomware, breaches, and Class Action lawsuits now becoming the norm, let alone shareholders demanding more transparency and holding Boards to account, it is all too easy to fall into the Not Secure trap, you may not get another chance. We have repeatedly called upon our government, the US and Australian governments via their DOD and several others to launch campaigns informing businesses of the dangers of being remiss when it comes to internet security. The examples I have used throughout this book offer a stark reminder of what ignoring internet facing and connected security can mean, and I have not even covered SOLARWINDS/SUNBURST yet the mother of them all, to date.

16

WWW.AVSVMCLOUD(.)COM (SOLARWINDS ATTACK) THE MODUS OPERANDI FOR ATTACKS SINCE STUXNET

An enthusiastic student can go on to become an expert when they continually apply themselves, sadly a complacent teacher may stay a teacher repeating the courses and cease growing, always remain a student.

In January 2010 officials of the International Atomic Energy Agency (IAEA) started noticing unusual occurrences at Natanz, the Iranian Nuclear Power facility, that had been under considerable scrutiny for some periods let alone having major concerns. In a bunker, over 50 feet underground, the bank of bright centrifuges was spinning at around 1,500 revolutions per second or 90,000 rpm. They had been working perfectly well for some two years enriching Uranium. The IAEA officials however noticed that a whole batch of centrifuges had been removed and were being replaced. The expected lifespan of a centrifuge is typically around ten years, and Natanz was relatively new and had just under 9,000 centrifuges. The number of failed centrifuges was abnormally high and raised concerns.

What the officials did not know at the time, nor did most of the world, and that included most of the US Intelligence agencies, was that in June 2009 Iran had been hit by a highly effective cyberattack in the shape of the world's first digital warhead to ultimately sabotage the Iranian Nuclear Power Program and the facility at Natanz. What the officials did not realise is that they were witnessing what would become to be known as the world's most sophisticated virus (at the time) ever discovered. A piece of software with no less than four Zero Days that had been honed since Project Aurora several years earlier, and many months of testing they would perfect the use and manipulation of digital code that would cause collateral damage and be known

DOI: 10.1201/9781003204145-16

for ever more as the World's first act of cyberwarfare and the world's first digital weapon, it would not be the last...

Those responsible and behind the global widespread intrusion into governments and corporate networks had exploited vulnerabilities and seams in the Iranian network's defences. The SolarWinds breach, known as SUNBURST, exploited all these elements and was not flagged on any of their cutting-edge security or systems. There had been more than a ten-year gap since Stuxnet and the SolarWinds attack (Sunburst), the similarities, and Modus Operandi bore amazing similarities... It has widely exposed the difference between the ability of Intelligence agencies and cyber providers, to lead offensive security and provide cybersecurity services to their clients. However, sadly the same cannot be said of their own defensive capabilities. General Paul Nakasone is considered by many as the US's top cyberwarrior and declared the battle against Russian interreference and infiltration had been managed and was under control only weeks ago on the actual day of the US election. Eight weeks later and the entire US intelligence agencies and government departments were completely consumed, and a majority was affected by the Russian infiltration of SolarWinds over the last nine months.

In March 2020, a hijacked, insecure, and unmanaged SolarWinds subdomain was taken over and repurposed and made secure again under Russian control, IP **20.140.0.1**. It used self-signing certificates to look legitimate and to avoid raising any concern. It had effectively commandeered the domain to gain privileges and access over time. The term Bradley Smith of Microsoft shared at the Senate Intelligence Committee was Domain Admin Access, in other words, total access and total control to move around as a SolarWinds team without fear of being spotted. It is suggested that an organisation typically averages six months before realising they have been breached. Ultimately, this enabled the attackers to gain full access to, and lace, SolarWinds's digital certificates with their own Sunburst malware. There are hundreds of reports on this breach at SolarWinds, the vast majority overlook the initial infiltration and access of the domain, none the less the actual malware was indeed sophisticated in a very similar way to Stuxnet had been over ten years earlier. The below timeline shows a chronological sequence of events the SolarWinds's breach went through. These events and timelines are compiled from various sources including the SEC, government agencies, Microsoft, Reuters, and Bloomberg. How the attack was discovered, the responses and activities from March 2020 to 31 December:

March to June 2020:

- **SolarWinds Attacked Without Knowing**: Two SolarWinds Orion software updates were quietly attacked. Hackers installed malware to ultimately spy on customers. Source: SolarWinds SEC filing, 14 December 2020.

Tuesday, 8 December 2020:

- **FireEye Suffers Attack**: FireEye discloses that state-sponsored hackers broke into FireEye's network and stole the company's Red Team penetration testing tools.

Wednesday, 9 December 2020: Note – the CEO transition plan and stock transactions mentioned below were announced two days before SolarWinds publicly announced the breach.

- **SolarWinds's CEO Transition**: The company discloses Sudhakar Ramakrishna will succeed Kevin Thompson as SolarWinds's President and CEO, effective 4 January 2021. The CEO announcement is made before FireEye apparently alerts SolarWinds about the breach two days later on 11 December. **Source**: Channel E2E.
- **SolarWinds Stock Transactions**: On the financial front, Canada Pension Plan Investment Board (CPP Investments) has made a $315 million secondary investment in SolarWinds. The deal involves CPP buying an existing stake from private equity firms Silver Lake and Thoma Bravo and their respective co-investors. The transaction disclosure is made before FireEye apparently alerts SolarWinds about the breach two days later on 11 December.

Friday, 11 December 2020:

- **FireEye Discovers SolarWinds Was Attacked**: During a FireEye breach investigation, FireEye discovers that SolarWinds Orion updates had been corrupted and weaponised by hackers.

Saturday, 12 December 2020:

- **FireEye Alerts SolarWinds CEO**: A FireEye executive advised SolarWinds CEO Kevin Thompson that Orion contained a vulnerability as the result of a cyberattack. **Source**: SolarWinds SEC filing, 17 December 2020.
- **Emergency National Security Council (NSC) White House Meeting**: The National Security Council (NSC) holds a meeting at the White House on Saturday to discuss a breach of multiple government agencies and businesses. The NSC is the US President's principal forum for considering national security and foreign policy matters with his senior national security advisors and cabinet officials. **Source**: Reuters, 13 December 2020.

Sunday, 13 December 2020:

- **CISA Emergency Directive**: The Cybersecurity and Infrastructure Security Agency (CISA), part of the US Department of Homeland Security, issues emergency directive 21-01, ordering federal agencies to power down SolarWinds Orion because of a substantial security threat. **Source**: MSSP Alert.
- **SolarWinds Security Advisory**: SolarWinds issues a Security Advisory outlining the Orion platform hack and associated defensive measures. **Source**: MSSP Alert.
- **FireEye Disclosure**: FireEye says an attacker has leveraged the SolarWinds supply chain to compromise multiple global victims. **Source**: FireEye.
- **Microsoft Guidance**: Microsoft offered this guidance regarding the attacks.
- **Media Coverage**: The initial report hinting at the SolarWinds Orion hack surfaces from Reuters. Hackers believed to be working for Russia have been monitoring internal email traffic at the US Treasury and Commerce departments, according to people familiar with the matter, adding they feared the hacks uncovered so far may be the tip of the iceberg.

Monday, 14 December 2020:

- **SolarWinds SEC Filing**: The software company discloses the breach in an SEC filing. **Source**: SolarWinds and the SEC.

- **SolarWinds Stock Falls**: Shares in $SWI fall about $20 on the breach news.

Tuesday, 15 December 2020:

- **Attack Victims**: The victims include the US Commerce and Treasury Departments; the Department of Homeland Security (DHS), the National Institutes of Health, and the State Department. **Source**: *The Wall Street Journal.*
- **Investigation Request**: A bipartisan group of six senators want the FBI and the Cybersecurity and Infrastructure Security Agency (CISA) to submit a report to Congress about the impact of the SolarWinds's cyberattack on agencies. The lawmakers want answers to six questions including how many agencies were impacted, how the FBI and CISA worked together to address the attack, and if agencies failed to implement FISMA or other cyber laws. The senators also want an additional briefing on the topics.

Wednesday, 16 December 2020:

- **SolarWinds MSP Update**: On the one hand, SolarWinds's MSP's software was not part of the attack. But on the other hand, the SolarWinds's MSP group is taking extra steps to mitigate risk currently. Specifically, SolarWinds MSP on 16 December told its partners that it will revoke digital certificates for its MSP tools and require customers to digitally re-sign into its products. SolarWinds will begin issuing the new certificates on 18 December and will revoke all its old certificates by 21 December **Source**: CRN, 17 December 2020.
- **Attack Kill Switch**: A key malicious domain name used in the attack has been commandeered by security experts and used as a 'killswitch.' **Source**: KrebsOnSecurity.
- New York Times **Editorial**: 'The magnitude of this national security breach is hard to overstate,' according to Thomas P. Bossert, former homeland security adviser to President Trump. **Source**: *The New York Times.*
- **FBI Investigation**: As the lead for threat response, the FBI is investigating and gathering intelligence to attribute, pursue,

and disrupt the responsible threat actors. **Source**: CISA, 16 December 2020.

- **Private Equity Statement About Stock Sales**: *The Washington Post* raised questions about private equity companies Thoma Bravo and Silver Lake Partners selling some SolarWinds shares ahead of the breach disclosure. However: 'Thoma Bravo and Silver Lake were not aware of this potential cyberattack at SolarWinds prior to entering into a private placement to a single institutional investor on 12/7.'

Thursday, 17 December 2020:

- **IT Service Providers Targeted**: Microsoft has discovered that more than 40 of its customers were targeted. Roughly 44% of those customers were IT service providers, software, or technology companies. Microsoft described the need for a 'strong and global cybersecurity response.'
- **Five IT solutions providers and consulting firms** – Deloitte, Digital Sense, ITPS, Netdecisions, and Stratus Networks – were breached earlier this year via the SolarWinds Orion vulnerability.
- **US Nuclear Agency Targeted**: Hackers accessed systems at the National Nuclear Security Administration, which maintains the US nuclear weapons stockpile. **Source**: Politico, 17 December 2020.
- **Microsoft Investigation**: 'We can confirm that we detected malicious Solar Winds binaries in our environment, which we isolated and removed. We have not found evidence of access to production services or customer data. Our investigations, which are ongoing, have found absolutely no indications that our systems were used to attack others.
- **White House Meetings**: The White House is meeting daily to discuss the SolarWinds Orion breach, attack victims, potential fallout, and a potential response.
- **SolarWinds Statement About Stock Sales, CEO Transition**: *The Washington Post* raised questions about private equity companies Thoma Bravo and Silver Lake Partners selling some SolarWinds shares ahead of the breach disclosure. However, SolarWinds said: 'In order to be as

clear as possible, we want to highlight that the exploration by SolarWinds of the potential spinoff of its MSP business and the departure of our CEO, were announced in August 2020. Finally, all sales of stock by executive officers in November were made under pre-established Rule 10b5-1 selling plans and not discretionary sales.' **Source**: SolarWinds SEC fining, 17 December 2020; *The Washington Post*, 15 December 2020.

- **US Cybersecurity Policy**: President-elect Joe Biden vowed to elevate cybersecurity as an 'imperative' when he takes office and said he would not 'stand idly by' in the face of cyberattacks following a massive breach that impacted the US government. President Trump has not publicly commented about the attack.

Saturday, 19 December 2020:

- **Trump Administration**: US Secretary of State Mike Pompeo blamed Russia for the SolarWinds Orion Sunburst hack that compromised numerous federal agencies and US corporations, while President Trump said he was sceptical of a growing consensus in Washington about the country's role. **Source**: *The Wall Street Journal*, 19 December 2020.
- **Who Got Hacked**: Roughly 198 organisations, overall, were hacked using the SolarWinds backdoor, according to Allan Liska, a threat analyst at Recorded Future.

Monday, 21 December 2020:

- **Statement – US Treasury Department**: The hack impacted the Treasury Department's unclassified systems, but the department has not seen any damage, Treasury Secretary Steven Mnuchin said in a CNBC interview on Monday. **Source**: Reuters, 21 December 2020.
- **Who Got Infected**: Organisations such as Cisco Systems, Intel, Nvidia, Deloitte, VMware, and Belkin had installed the infected SolarWinds Orion software, though it is unclear if the hackers actually took additional steps once the infected software found its way into those organisations.

Tuesday, 22 December 2020:

- **US Treasury Department Emails Compromised**: Dozens of email accounts at the Treasury Department were compromised with hackers breaking into systems used by the department's highest-ranking officials.

Wednesday, 23 December 2020:

- Crowdstrike earlier this year was targeted as part of the attack, but hackers did not enter Crowdstrike's systems.

Thursday, 24 December 2020:

- **Latest SolarWinds Statement and Patches**: SolarWinds summarised its latest patches and fixes for the Orion Supernova attack.

Wednesday, 30 December 2020:

- **Updated CISA Guidance**: The CISA updated its guidance on the SolarWinds Orion vulnerability. Specifically, all federal agencies' operating versions of the SolarWinds Orion platform other than those identified as 'affected versions' are required to use at least SolarWinds Orion Platform version 2020.2.1HF2. The National Security Agency (NSA) has examined this version and verified that it eliminates the previously identified malicious code. Given the number and nature of disclosed and undisclosed vulnerabilities in SolarWinds Orion, all instances that remain connected to federal networks must be updated to 2020.2.1 HF2 by COB 31 December 2020.

Thursday, 31 December 2020:

- Microsoft says Russian hackers viewed some of the software company's source code, but the hackers were unable to modify the code or get into Microsoft's products and services.

As I write, 3 January 2021, the full extent of this breach is far from known or realised. What is certain is the intelligence and government departments, including the US Treasury, are completely consumed by the breach and its current, consequential breaches and implications.

Figures being touted currently suggest this breach will cost in excess of $1 trillion. That eye-watering figure may well be vastly surpassed, and in truth, the cases of the DNC, Ukraine and multiple, systemic infiltration across numerous government departments, 2015 onwards, coupled with the intelligence confirmed and indeed warned about, would lead the majority of people to question why a company such as SolarWinds was allowed to act so negligently by ignoring their own security position but more specifically maintaining insecure subdomains which enabled initial infiltration. They, along with far too many of their clients, ignored basic internet facing security, best practices and created vast opportunities to be, not only targeted, but easily and successfully infiltrated and attacked. They made themselves, in essence, a sitting duck and for that must be held totally responsible. They and their clients made assumptions and all clients across the entire supply chain, both up and down, including the government, complicit by their inactions.

Laws and regulators, on the back of such cyberattacks, must define, and create vastly improved and effective, proper, fit for purpose cybersecurity. Shareholders can, and are now holding Boards to account, as in this SolarWinds and many other cases. Actions and indeed inactions accompanied by evidence and intelligence showing fundamental basics are continually ignored, even after the fact. Must find those culpable of negligence and held to account. SolarWinds and many of their clients had the very best cybersecurity capability and yet, through negligence and complacency, a single digital certificate could end up costing more than $1 trillion. The issue of Shareholders holding Boards to account is an interesting area. Thoma Bravo is a major shareholder of SolarWinds and sit on the Board. Thoma Bravo, the major Private Equity firm, decided to sell $millions, hundreds of $millions of stocks in SolarWinds only hours before the breach was formally disclosed. I am sure the SEC is looking into the timing and actions, however such actions could, and surely must be considered a conflict of interest.

This attack on SolarWinds has been universally accepted as the single, most detrimental attack on tens of thousands of organisations and the attack that simply keeps on being discovered. Wouldn't it be great to see lessons being learned by such oversight and negligence? Sadly, that simply is not the case. President Joe Biden and our Prime Minister Boris Johnson are allocating more funds to increase cyber capabilities and that cash is heading straight towards more offensive capabilities and Zero Days. We clearly learnt nothing from the Flame, Duqu, Stuxnet, EternalBlue, Wannacry, and Sunburst family of attacks. They all utilised known and manipulated network vulnerabilities and yet, our governments and IC are guilty of continuing to ignore the very same vulnerabilities in our own networks. Nowhere more so than where everyone is connected to the internet.

17
THE TAO, QUANTUM INSERT, AND OWN GOALS

'There are two types of companies: those that have been hacked, and those that will be' Robert Bueller, FBI Director 2012.

Although it is hard to disagree with the above statement with unreserved belief, what I can say is you can either roll over and wait to be easily attacked like a coward cowering in a corner or make yourself as secure and strong as possible. Incompetence and lack of good security are why so many companies are simply attacked, it is all too often a self-inflicted position. What is really interesting is that the US and UK governments seem hell bent on subscribing to the Deterrence Theory and like their stock of Nuclear Weapons are stock piling Zero Days at $1–1.5 million a time instead of ensuring basic security is in place and encouraged.

Formed as early as 1998 during the Clinton Administration, the Office of Tailored Access Operations (TAO), and later called Computer Network Operations (CNE), was a cyberwarfare intelligence-gathering unit of the National Security Agency (NSA). Its purpose was to identify, monitor, infiltrate, and gather intelligence on computer systems being used by entities, originally by foreign countries to the US. TAO is reportedly the largest and arguably the most important component of the NSA's huge Signals Intelligence Directorate (SIGINT), consisting of considerably more than 1,000 military and civilian computer hackers, intelligence analysts, targeting specialists, computer hardware, software designers, and electrical engineers. In 2013, a document leaked by the former NSA contractor Edward Snowden described the unit's work, confirming TAO has software templates allowing it to break into commonly used hardware, including routers, switches, and firewalls from multiple product vendor lines. TAO engineers prefer to tap networks rather than isolated computers, because there are typically many devices on a single

DOI: 10.1201/9781003204145-17

121

122   **STUXNET TO SUNBURST**

network and the metadata can be analysed. TAO focuses on metadata collection on a global, massive scale.

The Advanced Network Technology (ANT) catalogue is a 50-page classified document listing technologies available to the US National Security Agency TAO, by the ANT division to aid cyber surveillance. Most devices are described as already operational and available to US Intelligence nationals and also members of the Five Eyes alliance. According to *Der Spiegel*, which released the catalogue to the public on 30 December 2013, the list reads like a mail-order catalogue. One from which other NSA employees can order technologies from the ANT division for tapping their targets' data. The document was created in 2008. Security researcher Jacob Appelbaum gave a speech at the Chaos Communications Congress in Hamburg, Germany in 2013, in which he detailed techniques that the simultaneously published *Der Spiegel* article he co-authored disclosed from the catalogue.

Technologies, code-named QUANTUMSQUIRREL and FOXACID, for example allowed the ANT team to use The Onion Router (TOR) browser and exploit it by identifying other TOR users on the internet and then execute an attack against them via their Firefox web browser. Such attacks are known as CNE. First the NSA, via their massive monitoring of the internet, and agency's partnership with Telco firms, use fingerprinting detecting HTTP requests from the TOR network using systems such as XKEYSCORE. Other programs such as STORMBREW, FAIRVIEW, OAKSTAR, and BLARNEY were also used.

Using other powerful analytical tools with code names such as TURBULENCE, TURMOPIL, and TULMIT (there are hundreds) the NSA automated analysis looking for The Onion Router (TOR) connections to infiltrate. TOR is used for anonymity on the internet and all TOR users look the same, however different from other, regular internet users. By definition, and by using TOR, it is impossible to know who the user is and where they are based. Once a computer is attacked, it can call back to the Mothership using its network of secret internet servers to redirect those users to another set of servers. Ultimately, the NSA can pretty much do whatever it wants once they get to this position with a computer. Digital eavesdrop, connect to all other connected devices, divert all dataflow, gather, and harvest all intelligence and take over command and control. One can

THE TAO, QUANTUM INSERT, AND OWN GOALS 123

understand the irresistible and intoxicating new capability and control enjoyed by such clandestine tools and methods. As with many attacks, TOR itself is not attacked, but the vulnerabilities that Firefox browsers have are. This is a very similar situation in third-party supply chain attacks that literally, very few, possibly no one considers. We all know the saying, a chain is only as strong as its weakest link, well in security the situation is the same. A company is only as secure as the company's weakest security link within the digital trust ecosystem and supply chain. Consider Blackbaud's breach and the consequential breaches of over 125 other companies, charities, and universities. Likewise, for the recent SolarWinds's breach, it is far too early to say, however the tally of effected clients are in the tens of thousands and that will include many government organisations including the US Treasury.

QUANTUM INSERT (QI) was another code-named tool and method from the ANT handbook and has been used since 2005 by both the NSA and GCHQ to hack into what is perceived to be the highest value and hard to reach systems and implant malware. Such targets are not easy to reach via a phishing campaign. How QI works is by hijacking a browser as it is trying to access a web page forcing it to visit a malicious site instead. The attackers can then surreptitiously download malware directly onto the target's machine from the rogue web page. QI has been used to hack terrorists in the Middle East. It was also used in a highly controversial joint operation against the Belgian telecom company Belgacom and against workers of OPEC, the organisation of Petroleum exporting countries. Some 300 plants were made in and around 2010 and remained undetected according to the agency's own documents. Often common detection tools used at the time such as Snort, Bro, and Suricata could find the plants, however like many things, particularly in cyber breaches and attacks, it is imperative to be looking and ideally, knowing where to look. This is where most errors are made and by overlooking the fact a company has been infiltrated, often by numerous agencies, and cybercriminals alike, assumptions are being made and very few are looking.

History shows us clearly that the NSA and GCHQ have been working closely together over the last two decades infiltrating Networks, manipulating servers, planting, and abusing TLS/SSL and PKI, totally unbeknown to organisations. Should it come as any surprise that a SolarWinds's attack was just a matter of time? Absolutely not, in many ways, it is a surprise that it has taken over ten years. One could also argue many others may, and will also utilise the lessons they have learnt by the agency's previous and ongoing clandestine digital operations, and all in their quest for what they claimed was security.

In 2015, the NSA was exposed twice by Moscow and Kaspersky Labs who had published a report about the activities of The Equation Group detailing malware implanted in numerous companies and countries. The Equation Group was widely suspected of being nothing more than a branch of the NSA (TAO). Specifically, these exploits targeted enterprise firewalls, antivirus software, and Microsoft products. Some of the Kaspersky report detailed the groups technology including software used in Olympic Games (Stuxnet). Kaspersky updated their antivirus software to identify and address TAO's malware that removed the hack for some 400 million users and certainly did not endear themselves by doing so to the agencies.

The Shadow Brokers is a hacker group that first appeared in 2016. They published numerous leaks that contained hacking tools, including several Zero-Day exploits that the Equation Group had developed. The Shadow Brokers are a group of seemingly very competent individuals who work as brokers providing intelligence on hacking capabilities and tools. Their first leak was via Twitter on 13 August 2016 from the account @shadowbrokerss announcing a Pastebin page and a GitHub repository containing references and instructions for obtaining and decrypting the content of a file containing exploits from the Equation Group. The Pastebin introduced a section titled 'Equation Group Cyber Weapons Auction'. It was in effect an auction for tools that the Equation Group had developed to be sold to the highest bidder. The description went into some depth and included the term, Auction files better than Stuxnet. This was real-life digital espionage on a scale that was simply unbelievable and ensured a near level playing field of offensive digital weaponry to the highest bidder.

Other Shadow Broker files that have been sold include EternalBlue. Over 200,000 machines were infected with tools from this leak. In May 2017, the major WannaCry Ransomware attack used the EternalBlue exploit on Server Message Block to spread itself. The same exploit was used to help carry out the 2017 Petya cyberattack. EternalBlue contains kernel shellcode to load the non-persistent DoublePulsar backdoor.

THE TAO, QUANTUM INSERT, AND OWN GOALS   125

This allows the installation of PEDDLECHEAP payload which can then be accessed by the attacker using DanderSpritz software.

In October 2016, *The Washington Post* reported that Harold Martin, a former Booz Allen Hamilton contractor, had been accused of stealing 50 terabytes of data from the NSA. The Shadow Brokers continued posting cryptographically signed messages as well as interviews whilst Martin was detained. Remember, during this same period, the Democratic National Committee was being infiltrated continuously which resulted in a clean sweep of digital devices and the 2016 elections were looming. It must have been an incredibly frantic time for the US government and their agencies. The question which remains is who and how were all new devices authenticated at PKI level? Was the replacement of all technology merely a great commercial exercise, with limited long-term security benefits?

Looking at the DNC breach and the more recent SolarWinds's breach for a moment, the view that there was, and is, no option but to replace all servers, devices, and making a clean sweep of things being the only option is interesting as was undertaken following the breach at DNC. A question to ask then is how does any organisation know what is on each device, so far as certificates and encrypted keys are concerned? The servers, PCs, laptops, and so on. No one can undertake full discovery of all certificates and keys on any device, server, or digital device unless they have a proprietary technology such as Whitethorn® and we have not had any discussions with any of these organisations. How can the company that undertook the replacement and upgrades at the DNC, for example or those that might do so across the SolarWinds, and the extended breached organisations, provide total authentication and assurance that each device doesn't simply come complete with new backdoors, controlled or otherwise by the agencies or from the OEM? What devices will be used, where will they be manufactured, procured from, just who is providing such assurances. I may be being cynical here, however replacing compromised devices with new, but also quite likely compromised devices, is nothing short of foolish and will only prove to be a very expensive exercise to gain very little, possibly nothing. Just like the Russians and the IBM electronic computers that sent unencrypted messages before they were encrypted (plain text), new devices and internet connections, can, if not authenticated, perform the very same tasks.

126 STUXNET TO SUNBURST

What is abundantly clear is that during the Clinton, then Bush, and finally Obama's administration, security went from ensuring Homeland Security to full, complete surveillance and global digital exploitation and manipulation. The initial consideration was almost certainly and quite arguably, one to ensure that the US was secure and protected. Unfortunately, ultimate power got the better of the government and agencies and they demanded more and more from their clandestine Network Exploitation and PKI manipulation. Cyber intelligence morphed from data gathering and surveillance to become being used for offensive use and the creation of cyberwarfare using digital code in the form of Stuxnet/Olympic Games. Once these methods were unleashed, they quickly became re-engineered and adopted by other State Nations and cybercriminals. The tools, techniques, and exploitation methods and capabilities developed by our own agencies and governments were now being turned against us by our adversaries. Washington, the NSA, and GCHQ are truly struggling to defend against cyberattacks and have been for several years as the SolarWinds's breach clearly demonstrates. They have literally all fallen victims by having the Monster they created turned against them, our governments have no answers apart from continuing with the Deterrence Theory and threat which clearly has not worked to date. The assumptions made on the inability of Joe Public to ensure security enabled the networks and PCs to be constantly abused and manipulated by the agencies to perform their tasks and go unnoticed, are now the same people that are floundering as they are under attack from adversaries and looking for guidance, the governments and agencies have scored a massive own goal on this and how. Networks and PCs when connected to the internet can act like broken one-way valves, allowing unrestricted data flows, in and out of the OS.

What must be questioned is why the agencies are refusing organisations and even their own governments to truly benefit from what our team developed in the form of Whitethorn® for a NATO client. Every security professional knows, or should know, that the agency's utilised and manipulated TLS and SSL certificates and PKI to gain a digital advantage and that such actions and activity is widespread. Immaterial of one's views on secrecy and privacy (although there are clearly strong laws governing both) the weaknesses that were exploited within the system, a system they originally designed and developed is now under massive and constant attacks by our adversaries and they, along with millions of users, have no answer and yet they continue to deny the world, who could greatly benefit and gain visibility by using Whitethorn® enabling far greater control, management, and security. A term I use frequently is complacent or complicit and if our governments weren't seen to be offering a vaccine for Covid-19, there would be even more rioting, however they are not offering any solution for cyberattacks that are changing the global economic position and effecting millions of people daily.

18
THE COVID-19 BREACHES

The coronavirus is a large family of different viruses. Some cause common cold-like symptoms, others can infect animals, including bats, camels, and cattle. But more specifically, how did SARS-CoV-2, the new coronavirus, cause Covid-19 to start? The virus was first detected in Wuhan, China in late 2019 and set off a global pandemic. Experts suggest SARS-Cov-2 originated in bats, according to the Middle East respiratory Syndrome (MERS) and Severe Acute Respiratory Syndrome (SARS) bodies. It is commonly believed that SARS-CoV-2 made the jump to humans at one of Wuhan's open air wet markets where live animals are slaughtered for human consumption. Crowded conditions and questionable sanitation potentially created the perfect situation. There are other conspiracy theories; however, this is the theory believed to be correct, at least by these two leading and highly respected organisations. For the record, the first identification of a human coronavirus dates to 1965 by scientists, it caused a common cold. Later that decade, researchers discovered a group of similar viruses which took their name by their crown-like appearance.

As Covid-19 spread, both domestically and internationally, it became known that it was transmitted from person to person. For a little over 12 months the world was effectively put on hold due to the pandemic as the world focused on remediation and vaccination. As of 3 January 2021, the World Health Organisation (WHO) confirmed that there were 83,322, 449 Covid-19 cases and some 1,831,412 related deaths. Of that number those that were infected are as follows: 36 million were in the Americas, 26 million in Europe, 12 million in South East Asia, nearly 5 million in the Eastern Mediterranean, nearly 2 million in Africa, and just over 1 million in the Western Pacific. The Covid-19 virus spreads primarily through droplets of saliva or discharge from the nose when an infected person sneezes or coughs. Respiratory etiquette has been encouraged, and subsequently enforced across the globe pretty much without exception.

DOI: 10.1201/9781003204145-18

As of yesterday, over 75,000 people had died in the UK due to Covid-19 and the number of people being infected a day is more than 50,000. That number has risen to over 100,000 deaths in the UK within three weeks, that is the end of January 2021. The latest strain of the virus is acknowledged as being more infectious causing more contamination. Even though tighter social distancing and lockdown tiering structures have been put in place making the end of 2020 a rather more sombre event in comparison to the same period to just a year ago, just after the virus was first discovered. Estimates of the global and economic impacts are substantial and a recent article jointly written by Lord Nick Stern and Professor Tim Besley, both members of DELVE, a multidisciplinary group convened by the Royal Society, concluded their report by saying; 'In any economic and social shock, the best course of action is to take immediate steps towards long-term recovery, rather than waiting.' The Covid-19 crisis has been an urgent wake-up call for the future preparations and for future recurrence of any epidemic – and for future possible coronaviruses – will be repaid by helping to mitigate the impact on schools, the NHS, public transport and supply chains, and the economy. We must recognise and act on the fragilities of old, outdated systems.

In October 2020, the International Monetary Fund (IMF) produced a report and estimated that the global economy, due to Covid-19 in 2020, would reach $28 trillion in lost output. That is nearly one-third of the global total output. Gita Gopinath, the IMF's economic counsellor, described coronavirus as the worst crisis since the Great Depression and said the pandemic would leave deep and enduring scars causing job losses, weaker investment, and children being deprived of education. The Covid-19 pandemic cannot be underestimated in its terms of a catastrophe on all counts.

Earlier in the year, in April 2020, we had already commenced our research across a number of prominent companies both here in the UK and the US. The Health and Education sectors were just two areas we were researching. Late in April and into May, we had been researching UK's leading Universities, and with the pandemic now looking considerably worse than any government had originally believed, or indeed hoped, we knew we would all be working from home for some considerable time (this book is a direct result). I

THE COVID-19 BREACHES

131

will refrain from adding my personal view on the handling of the pandemic, it certainly was an 'unprecedented' situation as we have been reliably informed on hundreds of occasions, the word has almost become worn out. However, as we all now know, more lives could, potentially have been saved if we had actioned and adopted stricter policies sooner. Covid-19 was certainly not going to be a regular inconvenience like the common flu. We decided to research the largest and most prominent Universities such as Oxford, Cambridge, London School of Economics (LSE), and so on. Oxford alone received around £120 million per year in research grants and scientists were actively working on Covid-19 research. Unbeknown to us at the time, Oxford University was working with AstraZeneca who, coincidentally recently launched the Oxford/AstraZeneca vaccine and has been made available for the first time. Imagine then our surprise seeing Oxford and the LSE maintaining suboptimal homepages due to invalid, obsolete TLS/SSL digital certificates that had expired many months beforehand. Such a situation rendered Oxford and the LSE not only targets, but targets that could be easily breached. Clearly none of the research funding monies of £120 million was being used to secure the University, nor was any other for that matter. We emailed several times, called and just short of hounding Oxford University, tried to get their attention to alert them. We knew just how vulnerable they were and how valuable the data and PII data they held on file would be. Oxford alone has 24,000 students and received seven applicants for each available place. Oxford also employs around 15,000 staff so in total, in any one year, it will manage the PII data of some 183,000 people. In addition to this, Oxford was leading the charge, so far as UK Academia is concerned, on a vaccine for Covid-19. We were truly shocked by our findings; however, there it was www.ox.ac.uk as a Not Secure homepage and for many months. Our research found similar situations across a large percentage, including the governing bodies of the Higher Education, and when we researched Colleges as part of an extended programme, we found the same, inadequate, and woeful lack of security across a large percentage of Further Education (FE). The Oxford domain eventually received a Let's Encrypt three-month cert in September 2020, a full five months after receiving our first note. It sounds a similar story to the FBI Special Agent Adrian Hawkins and his efforts and timelines when he tried to warn the DNC that they were being breached. It took him six months, maybe our voice is a just tad louder as it seemingly took one month less…

There was much worse to come. On 11 May 2020, the British supercomputer Archer was breached. Originally it was suggested and reported in the media, that it had been breached, along with subsequent European supercomputers, for digital, cryptocurrency mining. This turned out to be something of a red herring as it was later confirmed that www.archer.ac.uk was indeed breached by Russia, and also possibly China to infiltrate and to extract research on Covid-19 vaccine and all associated research. The same situation had also been found to be the case across other European supercomputers that had also been hacked. All supercomputers required swapping out SSH keys, however SSHs themselves are unable to discover all SSH keys. We offered to assist as Whitethorn® can easily find and replace all SSHs. We did not hear back. Immediately after the breach of Archer was announced, we undertook, as usual, full research. We pretty much immediately discovered the homepage was being maintained as Not Secure, the digital certificate having expired in April several weeks prior to Archer being breached. Was this coincidence, could academia seriously be so systemically negligent? It was certainly starting to seem to be more than just incompetence. I informed the Professor at Edinburgh University where Archer was based and whom I know. He confirmed 'Academics aren't great at security or the basics. I also informed the CEO of Cray the supercomputers manufacture, who simply said, and I quote, 'Thanks.' It was later discovered that the criminals had accessed the computer itself by exploiting the login nodes, forcing the EPCC systems to disable access to the systems. We called, emailed, and tried every way possible, including emailing the webmaster, to no avail to inform them as we had done with Travelex and many others. We screenshot everything, this enables us to avoid any confusion later and for our records, it also saves any contentious position at a later stage should there be any reason for legal proceedings to evidence negligence or even sometimes, foul play. So, several weeks later and post breach, we checked Archer and it was showing that it now, miraculously had a valid certificate and rather strangely, it had been backdated to a date pre the breach. This was clearly to cover up the fact it had been Not Secure pre and during the breach. Maybe there was an ulterior motive, it certainly was most unusual

THE COVID-19 BREACHES

133

and totally an unacceptable action. Unfortunately for whomever was trying to shoehorn in another, backdated certificate, the certificate chain would not accept it, so it remained Not Secure. Sometime later that certificate was removed altogether and believe it or not, even after the manipulation of SolarWinds's certificates, Archer remains Not Secure a full seven months after it was breached www.archer.ac.uk as is www.epcc.ed.ac.uk You could not make it up. As a footnote, Archer.ac.uk has now ceased even though the website is still active and still showing Not Secure. Archer2.ac.uk is now in its place. We will of course research this later.

We were more than a tad concerned with the findings (foul play could not be ruled out) from our initial reports and decided to look further whilst at the same time trying to raise the alarm. Our concerns were based around the vast humanitarian knock on effects. The research could easily have been stolen, even in part, replicated, and uncontrolled and then falsely distributed via a more than willing and demanding grey market. We had already witnessed the Personal Protective Equipment (PPE) rush. Such a falsely acknowledged and supposedly tested vaccine could find its way into the vaccine supply chain, when in fact it may only be a poor substitute with a cocktail of partial research and substitute ingredients. Covid-19 had unquestionably created a vast, dynamic market and demand, one only had to see the PPE, testing and masks' supply and costs multiply many times over and supplier numbers go through the roof. It was fraught with opportunity, and fraught with danger. The huge implications, as the numbers of people affected, and fatalities above clearly were showing. Research last year by the Institute of Economic Affairs (IEA) found that when they procured samples via the internet, 16% had dexamethasone and 18% had hydroxychloroquine failing the spectrometer. The number of fakes was far higher than even Viagra suggesting that there would be a major and incredibly dangerous problem when other cures and vaccines were made available. This week, a ninety-two-year-old lady in the UK paid a door knocking conman claiming he had a vile of Covid-19 vaccine for £160. She then paid him and allowed him to inject her there and then with what we have yet to find out. The implications for human life could not be more serious.

We started research with the main pharmaceutical companies and reached out to Moderna, Pfizer, Astra Zeneca, and of course Oxford

University as all had, or still had, suboptimal internet facing security meaning they could easily be infiltrated; indeed, they may well have already been as the sector is one of the worse rated sectors to be cyberattacked and that was even before Covid-19. Archer had been breached in May, and the European Medicines Agency (EMA) was also subsequently breached in December 2020. Our research across all companies showed inadequate security along with a plethora of expired, unmatched, and broken certificate chains, HTTP sites, weak cipher, TLS 1.0, and so on. Security was clearly not an issue or focus and these companies were all extremely influential in the sanctioning, manufacture, and distribution of vaccines globally. Just like the 2016 US elections and most of our research and trying to get companies to action and remove their vulnerabilities, no one seems to want to listen, or care. A Covid-19 vaccine or vaccines would enable the world to get back on track, let alone potentially save hundreds of thousands, even millions of lives. Our research continued and in late November, the US distribution company Americold, who had already been contracted to distribute the new vaccine, was breached by Ransomware. It did not take too much to join the dots up, from research, to sanctioning, from production, to distribution, at all points, someone somewhere had been breached and our research showed many still had inadequate security and clearly were not addressing security even though the pandemic was a global game-changing event where IP and data theft was not only considered but predicted. None of it made sense, I am sure it may do in time.

In the summer of 2020, we also undertook a healthcare security research programme and researched some of the top 1,000 healthcare providers in the US. The healthcare centres will ultimately be providing personal vaccination as well as traditional healthcare in addition to their increase in care due to the Covid-19 pandemic. Numerous healthcare operators had already been hit by cyberattacks and already paid out substantial Ransomware sums. Again, given the situation and already well-known vulnerabilities, it should have been made a priority to ensure at least basic security was in place, yet sadly time after time this simply was not the case. The extensive research showed a systemic case of woefully inadequate security facing and connected to the internet. Such a position encouraged any cybercriminal to easily identify and launch an attack against an

THE COVID-19 BREACHES

incredibly weakly protected target. Cybercriminals do not have any qualms about people losing their livelihood. For that matter, they have no qualms about people losing their lives. They simply look at a target and undertake reconnaissance and attack insecure, easy targets. The Healthcare sector fits their MO as far as too many other sectors do also. One such Healthcare centre is www.uhnj.org who suffered a cyberattack in August 2020 and paid $675k Ransomware just a week later to get back their data and encryption keys for their own data from the cybercriminals. When I asked our research team to check, they found that the University Hospital of New Jersey was maintaining a completely Not Secure homepage. I connected with their CEO Shereef Elnahal, and subsequently sent several messages alerting him to their insecure position and situation which had been like it for several months and quite likely, the reason they had been targeted in the first place. He never answered once and even worse, here we are on 4 January 2021 and it remains Not Secure several months later. In other words, the data behind the homepage was not encrypted and lacked integrity. It could be breached again at any time. It is beyond belief that free advice and warnings can be and are continually ignored. By ignoring the basics and PKI, just as I was at 176 mph when I hit the near boiling engine oil, and then the Armco barrier, clients are little more than passengers and have zero control.

$billions and $billions are being wasted on false security endeavours only to be undermined, vulnerable, and then exploited due to basic security being overlooked or ignored. Let's sell AI, Quantum Computing, Smart Cities, and so on, when they are breached, and they will be, the scale and frequency will make the recent SolarWinds's breach look like a mere nuisance.

19

SHOULD WE BE CONCERNED OR WORRIED? OUR GOVERNMENT AND AGENCIES HAVE GOT THIS

Throughout November 2020, I approached the Technical Director of NCSC the face of GCHQ, Dr Ian Levy and sent several emails following our connecting on LinkedIn and to share our ongoing research and findings that we believed, unequivocally, effectively put National Security at risk. Dr Ian Levy kindly provided his NCSC email and requested we use that medium for all correspondence, which I did.

Eventually I received a response to my email which I was grateful for. For those that do not know me well, I am Black and White, I have no issues calling things exactly as they are. Of course, I always remain professional and always dignified. I am equally happy to have lunch with the ex-head of MI5 and have done so and developed a strong mutual friendship and reciprocal respect. At the same time however, if there is negligence and poor security, I will carefully consider the situation and then address it. I have never considered myself a very good dancer though… I never tend to shoot from the hip, however. I was very eager to provide insight to the NCSC as I had already done to the Australian DOD and the FBI of exactly how our solution Whitethorn® could be used to dramatically reduce the plethora of service outages and in general, consistent mayhem that poor controls and management of PKI and digital certificates and encrypted keys were causing. By providing discovery control, management and most importantly, visibility, PKI could, for the first time in history, be managed and managed well, we believed such a turnaround of capability, instead of the Wild West, would create a U-Turn in the war of cyberattacks and losses… Remember Whitethorn® was primarily developed to use multi-scanning capability to dig deep into systems

DOI: 10.1201/9781003204145-19

137

to find all TLS, SSL, PGP, and SSH certificates and keys within a breached NATO military installation and as such is totally unique in its capability. Talk of a Blackthorn version was a non-starter.

In the exchange of emails, I requested if Dr Levy could review and comment upon a redacted Whitethorn Shield® report to demonstrate our and its ability. It would also enable us to elaborate upon its granularity and capability and his professional view would be extremely useful as I appreciated his unquestionable knowledge and expertise. His response after kindly receiving and reviewing was as follows:

Certainly, the scan below doesn't look good, but the main one for me is an expired certificate. From a very quick look, I'd expect almost all the rest to be context specific and not necessarily an issue. There may be a perfectly good reason why they're running old software. I've not checked whether that version is formally supported. Many of the vulns you've listed require the feature to be enabled and you may have (eg) a transparent WAF in front of this which mitigates a bunch of stuff. And so on. So, yes, if this was a government department, I'd go have a word to see what was going on.

In another exchange, Dr Levy said:

We disagree about the causality of the relationship between weak website posture and breach. Having been involved in all of the big incidents that affect the UK, I don't believe that there is any evidence to show the causality. We do seem to agree that weak website posture is a possible (weakly correlated) indicator of wider security malaise.

I can only guess Dr Levy had not been involved in the agencies' earlier use of their own tools and methods under the code name of Quantum Insert, Flying Pigs, or Hush Puppies then...

The final exchange, below was my email dated 7 December, the day before the breach of SolarWinds was announced to the world by FireEye and the fact that a Russian attack had used an insecure website to gain access (Domain Hijacking and Takeover) to commandeer the site and then to stand up to www.avsvmcloud.com, the attackers then gained access and privileges. Ultimately, they managed to get access to, and lace SolarWinds's digital certificates with Sunburst,

SHOULD WE BE CONCERNED OR WORRIED? **139**

their highly developed malware. All this was totally unbeknown to SolarWinds and all SolarWinds's clients who then, unknowingly downloaded the malware. This breach is acknowledged, even after just one month, to be one of the world's most devastating, single breaches and will affect tens of thousands of clients including the government and US Treasury.

In one of my emails to Dr Levy, I wrote the following:

Dear Dr Levy

Many thanks for your email.

The attached article will be officially published tomorrow and share what Not Secure domains actually means.

It is not our intention to joust with you or any other agency, I believe we actually share the same desired outcome and immaterial of one's own personal views, the fact remains that adversaries are using internet access to identify, target and attack organisations. The fact so many ignore internet security simply makes the attacks easier and more plentiful. Just imagine what these ill-gotten gains are doing to bolster organised crime.

I completely agree, some of the report's findings can only ever be implied vulnerabilities, however, the MOD, NCSC, DOD, RAF, Royal Navy, British Army and many more have expired and insecure domains. That, as your comment confirms, is concerning and unacceptable. It is exactly why our findings are incredibly useful as by being proactive we are clearly showing weaknesses and vulnerabilities that should not be the case and that is particularly important at Government level. There is much room for improvement and imagine, if our personal beliefs and difference of opinions on the importance of such a position is more our thinking than yours? Either way, our findings simply cannot be dismissed. No one, no company, government or agency should be managing internet facing domains that are insecure as we both acknowledge jeopardising the entire domain eco system and business.

Finally, we have spent an inordinate amount of time trying to assist and I understand projects such as PRISM, XKEYSCORE, HUSH PUPPY and FLYING PIG using SSL and TLS for Network Exploitation may go against the grain to start encouraging the provision of full PKI visibility, controls and management, however just to confirm, the UK and the US are actually losing the cyberwar and seemingly have little defence. Everything has been tried and cracks smoothed over apart from proper PKI, certificate and key controls and management.

Our paper on the Covid-19 security from breached organisations, Pharmaceutical companies maintaining insecure current positions and distribution organisations being breached is shockingly concerning equally.

Best regards

Andy

A case study of the company based in Delaware within the attached paper sent to the NCSC could have been written as if it was SolarWinds and possibly more importantly, provided an overview of methods and tools the NSA and GCHQ had used for many years to infiltrate corporates and other governments to gain digital eavesdropping, the difference now, it was being use the same, but to infiltrate and exfiltrate for nefarious use. The exchange of emails with the Technical Director was responsive as it would appear, we both do a 14 hour plus day and most weekends. There may have been a day or so delay between exchanges, however, possibly this email struck a chord as I never received a response and some four weeks later, it seems as if I may not. Not even acknowledgement of a HNY reply wish via LinkedIn. We are on the same side, aren't we?

As you read through this book, it is all too easy to draw conclusions, beds have been made and people must sleep on them, none of that help our cause, and more importantly, reduces or beats cybercrime. The CNI organisation used lack of accountability and plausible deniability due to GCHQ's sway and influence even after showing Russian and Chinese presence, woefully poor controlled PKI, and a National Security position that placed the company, its dependants, and customers in real danger. Tier 1 Banks, major FS organisations, UK FS governing bodies, and think tanks have also been influenced by government agencies, but why? It is widely known that the agencies have utilised Computer Network Exploitation (CNE) for many years and inserted more TLS and SSL certificates than they care to, or in fact can remember, and quite possibly could no longer find. We know that our adversaries now have the same resource capability and

SHOULD WE BE CONCERNED OR WORRIED? 141

even, by being educated and buying tools and methods developed by our own agencies, have similar, and possibly some unique capability. The market for Zero-Day exploits is fiercely fought over and by virtually every government globally. If it were a sport, it would be called cheating.

We equally know that an attack only needs a single access point, such as our ongoing and highlighted website insecurity (where connections are made and being accessed). We also know that through TLS/SSL manipulation, first used to create the world's first digital weapon, Stuxnet, and now to carry one of the world's largest breaches at SolarWinds as in Sunburst. So, the question that one might want to pose is, why might any agency not want PKI and certificates to be made visible enabling proper control and management and vastly reducing the attack surface and breaches? It may be a question that never gets an answer; however, I can guarantee, we have witnessed over the last decade, the use of digital certificates to hide malicious code to launch cyberattacks and in December 2020, we witnessed the use of digital certificates to once again, carry malicious code to launch a devastating cyber breach at the very heart of the US and the US government. Unequivocally, such attacks will continue and utilise domain insecurity and digital certificates and go unnoticed until the infiltration surfaces as an outright breach.

After indirect communications with the NSA, I can report, and rather in a satisfactorily way, they have finally launched, heavily biased by our research and findings, their version of Obsolete TLS protocols management. In other words, website insecurity due to invalid certificates. It is one hell of a milestone and one that we are delighted with. It also validates everything we have been saying over the last several years.

https://www.nsa.gov/News-Features/Feature-Stories/Article-View/Article/2462345/nsa-releases-eliminating-obsolete-transport-layer-security-tls-protocol-configu/

Since PKI was adopted globally and the Certificate Authorities such as RSA were put in place, governments, via their agencies, have sought to manipulate it and given the fact Joe Public simply unknowingly accepted the certificates from the suppliers without question, literally from the day of PKI's inception, it has been manipulated by the agencies and corrupted. It has been, ever since used extensively by

142 STUXNET TO SUNBURST

the agencies for more and more clandestine operations. The terrorist attacks of 9/11 received more support for the agencies' projects as justice or was that revenge, which was sought, even though there were clearly many failings. That may be human instinct, however, over the last 20 years, the advantage that was once enjoyed by our governments and agencies to supposedly provide security, often at the cost of privacy, has now undergone a full turnaround and is now being used against all of us by our adversaries. The dilemma for our agencies and governments must be, do we now confirm what everyone has suspected and believed for years like our ownership of Crypto AG and Omnisec that built in backdoors to 120 governments and allies, and try to clean things up before the next SolarWinds breach, that is possibly imminent and possibly even bigger.

Actually, possibly much bigger as I shared with David Sanger of the *New York Times* that could, if breached, make the SolarWinds breach look a nuisance phone call by comparison, or to continue ignoring the real issues and the fact no answers are forthcoming out of the agencies to combat the digital attacks that they perfected and are now having used against them. Or are they relying on the Deterrence Theory and the threat of pulling out the Fat Man the last bastion?

20
MAKING THE MATTER FAR WORSE (IoT AND 5G)

Over the last several years, the world has witnessed an insatiable demand for the Internet of things (IoT) devices for simplicity and to enable on demand information and convenience. This has however come at a huge price including privacy compromises and dangers. Unlike laptops, personal computers, and phones, IoT devices are short of processing power and as such, that means they often have poor, or even no security, a tad like the first batch of the first PCs. We have become a world demanding functionality at the cost of sidelining privacy and in turn, security. In truth, if you went back 20–30 years, those Special Agents charged with espionage would have literally killed to be able to put, let alone plant a device, a microphone, speaker, or camera in full view and enable them to capture everything that went on. Indeed, they went to great lengths to gain such intelligence. People now actually pay and choose to do this! Digital doorbells and cameras are being hacked and spying on children playing and gaining insights to entire neighbourhoods, collecting data which can then be used for nefarious purposes down the line and very few even batter an eyelid. It makes security insanely tough, if not impossible to achieve. It was only this week that an Irish Education Governing body revealed that Paedophiles had infiltrated a school's online lesson via Microsoft Teams and the young children subjected to perverts performing lude acts instead of interacting and viewing their normal online lesson. Similarly, laptops being supplied by the UK government to school children had Russian Malware already implanted. These instances are the tip of the iceberg as the government, and indeed many organisations, run no checks whatsoever on digital equipment. It is new, out of the box, what can possibly go wrong.

Existing standards are woefully lacking and often simply non-existent and vendors are rarely, often not in any way incentivised to

DOI: 10.1201/9781003204145-20

144   STUXNET TO SUNBURST

ensure security. The world's population seemingly cannot buy IoT devices quickly enough and by doing so, add increasing collaboration among attackers. The unequivocal consensus is that IoT devices are undersecured and present a catastrophic security risk to all companies, however by continuing to ignore their inadequate security it is convenient. Gartner estimated that by the end of 2020 there would be 21 billion IoT devices in use up from 5 billion in 2015. Some 8 billion will be devices used in the industrial sector creating more opportunities to gain intelligence for hackers with nefarious intent. Chris Moyer CTO and VP at DXC said; 'For some, it seems like a slow-motion wreck playing out in real time. The reason the industry hasn't backed off is the value proposition is very powerful.' In other words, people were making money, who gave a hoot about security, sound familiar?

There is a common theme throughout the history of computing. When the first batch of personal computers (PCs) was shipped, no security was ever considered or offered. The new world of computing was about functionality. Sometime later, an executive thought they should think about security given the amount of PCs they were selling. So, the next batch of thousands of PCs were indeed shipped with a code for security, security was being taken so seriously that all PCs were shipped with the same code. Security has always and sadly, may always, play second fiddle to functionality as the massive sale of IoT devices clearly shows. The same can be said of most of the software and organisations. As mentioned earlier, the internet is currently being used for the good but equally, facilitating the illegal, and quite possibly with an out of kilter balance. This year it is predicted for every $ spent online, $2 will be lost to cybercrime. That is simply a crazy, and an unsustainable position. The powers that be are, including the tech giants, directly, inadvertently facilitating this position. I cannot therefore disagree with Robert Hannigan's (GCHQ) comment in 2016 whereby he said, 'However much they may dislike it, they have become the Command-and-Control networks of choice for terrorists and criminals' speaking of the Silicon Valley tech giants. The part he failed to confirm is that they, and their counterparts at the NSA, were doing the same and one of his major tasks after supporting No. 10 Downing Street and Tony Blair was to actively bring GCHQ into the 21st century and to increase the already extremely compromised Network Exploitation.

MAKING THE MATTER FAR WORSE (IOT AND 5G) 145

5G has a similar position. Further developed but still relying on much of the original technical capability of 2G, 3G, and 4G, 5G was still Not Secure but being relied upon more and more, it was being heralded as the communication capability coupled with greatly improved security. I spoke with the CEO of O2 Telefonica Mark Evans following their breach in late 2018 which was due to an unmanaged and unknown Ericson obsolete certificate. The O2 network was unavailable for most of the day including the Emergency Services who were under contract with O2 (imagine such a situation during Covid-19). Numerous organisations were effectively shut down also so far as voice and messaging was concerned. Many people had already migrated from fixed to mobile. Softbank was one such company. The digital certificate as usual took several hours to identify and then replace before service was resumed. All parties were rather embarrassed, not for the first time, and a meeting was set up with our team of PKI experts. Mark's right-hand man, the lady in charge of PKI, and a PKI engineer were confirmed for a meeting for January after the holidays.

We met with the team at their 260 Bath Road office in Slough. Our team consisted of our CIO, Chief Scientist, and me. We had swapped some preliminary details so the meeting could be as constructive as possible. The certificate and disruption to the business, let alone liability and costs would prove to be in their £millions. It quickly became apparent that the O2 PKI team was somewhat overwhelmed by the job they were trying to do and had very limited knowledge of what actual certificates made up their PKI let alone those of and the impact they might experience of their third-party supply chain of which Ericson was just one. I have told this story several times before and always received the same response of disbelief. However, when we elaborated on full PKI discovery and identification, control and management of all certificates and therefore preventing any future service outages as just experienced, the lady in charge of PKI declared; 'That won't happen again as I have a plan, I will be putting validity dates on all known certificates for 30 years plus, that way they will not expire during my tenure and thereafter, I simply will not care'... To say this shocked us and should have shocked O2 is a vast understatement. The fact she did not know what certificates made up their PKI or their third-party suppliers seemed to have been forgotten and O2 Telefonica took her logic and remain in a highly vulnerable and precarious position to this day by taking no further action. That year Mark Evans was awarded a CEO of the year award and O2 lost the Emergency services contract being won by Everything Everywhere, formerly Orange and now BT. This contract loss, worth tens of £millions, may be a direct result of the disruption and outage, however the Mobile Network Operator (MNO) market is another that is woefully insecure and totally ignorant of their PKI and lacks PKI controls and management.

The MNO market has fallen foul of service outages and breaches over the years and on multiple occasions. No MNO has any idea what their PKI looks like and many have considered looking, but never had the technology or capability, so they have chosen a huge box of Band Aid plasters to hand and taken a reactive stance. Security simply cannot be reactive. One such breach at www.three.com occurred on 29 October 2019 and was reported by users taking to social media that the Three website gave casual browsers the ability to access PII data. Users continued voicing their concerns on social media. The Register publication reported the breach in the media. Three UK is bound by Regulation 5a of the Privacy and Electronic Communications Regulations to explain exactly how many people were affected and what they were doing to respond to the breach. The same regulation required Three to notify all those effected by the breach without delay, however Three was very slow to act. Furthermore, our research showed that shortly after the breach, Three's homepage was being maintained as a Not Secure site due to PKI issues and an invalid certificate. My three (coincidence) emails to Three's CEO from June 2020 onwards to alert him of the insecure position were all ignored, although they had been read and today, 5 January 2021, the homepage remains Not Secure and against all PII regulations and GDPR is actively selling and taking payments and providing no security for their customers. So Three has continually ignored their security and position, and that of their customers. This has continued pre and post the last breach in October 2019 and for over 14 months. Three has over 130 million registered customers globally, whose security is quite possibly also compromised. This is in total contravention of UKDPA and GDPR regulations and yet they continue taking internet orders, payments in complete disregard to the company or its clients. Where are the ICOs on this?

MAKING THE MATTER FAR WORSE (IOT AND 5G)   147

On 21 May 2019, the BBC reported a breach of TalkTalk, another MNO whereby customers' details were found online available for anyone to capture the personal and sensitive PII data. TalkTalk had failed to inform 4,545 customers that their PII data, that was part of an earlier breach in 2015, they had been breached, furthermore, TalkTalk had informed the same clients that their details were not compromised providing an incorrect and misleading position. The 2015 breach saw the details of some 157,000 customers' details accessed including bank account details and other PII data. At the time, the Information Commissioner Office (ICO) investigated the breach and found multiple failings in TalkTalk's security process. As a reflection of the seriousness of the event, the ICO fined TalkTalk a record fine of £400,000. In the OFCOM 2019 poll, TalkTalk service was at the very bottom of their annual poll for service. Hardly surprising, customers effected by the hack had experienced numerous fraudulent, ongoing attacks as a direct result of the TalkTalk breach. On 19 November 2018, two cybercriminals, Matthew Hanley and Connor Allsopp, were found guilty and jailed for their attack on TalkTalk's website (internet facing) that cost a staggering £77 million and were jailed for 12 and eight months, respectively, I would question if the punishment was commensurate with the crime and associated costs and losses? In May 2017 the CEO, Dido Harding, stood down following the breach and left the company. She said,

> After seven extraordinary and fulfilling years, during which we have transformed TalkTalk's customer experience and laid the foundations for long term growth, I've decided it's time for me to start handing over the reins at TalkTalk and focus more on my activities in public service.

This quote was in total contradiction of OFCOMS findings and polls from 2016 to 2019 and customers voicing their outrage on social media and leaving in their droves to alternative MNOs. In May 2020, there was uproar when Dido Harding, the disgraced TalkTalk CEO, was appointed to lead the government's Covid-19 testing programme. Dido Harding was made a baroness during her time at TalkTalk in 2014 and is married to David Cameron's good friend and Conservative Party member John Penrose. The breach was greatly covered up at

TalkTalk to the anger of many and it eventually became known that the breach was directly via their website and that those customers that were breached, TalkTalk had stored their data in unencrypted form, in other words, in plain text as happens when a website is Not Secure by not having a valid certificate. The very same issue as www.three. com has, and had during its breach and shockingly, remains insecure to this day some 15 months later. Such lax security is the main reason cyber breaches occur and CEOs, Boards, and Executives must be held accountable if security is ever to be taken seriously.

T-Mobile, another MNO, only this week suffered a data breach which exposed thousands of phone numbers and call records on 3 January 2021 making them the third out of four major US MNOs to get hacked within the last 12 months. T-Mobile has assured customers their PII data has not been compromised and was not affected by the data breach, time will tell, I guess. TalkTalk had said the same in 2015. It is too early to comment further on this breach, however according to those involved, access was gained to servers (internet facing) and specifically gained access to Customer Proprietary Network Information (CPNI). This data supposedly only contains phone numbers and call-related data records. Of course, a connected server and some clever lateral movement once accessed has been gained, can provide further data including all PII data and much more besides. Again, time will tell however our brief research on T-Mobile security facing the internet, showed a far from ideal position. Clearly T-Mobile is no stranger to data infiltration.

It was not that long ago in 2012 when Cybereason reported that at least a dozen mobile carriers from across the world reported they were under attack, and control by hackers that could shut down the mobile network creating a partial or even total blackout. The Boston security company had discovered that Chinese hackers were holding tons of data by taking controls of databases of most of the phone network providers operating in Asia, Africa, Europe, and North America along with the Middle East. Hundreds of gigabytes of data had been accessed, and if made public, the activity could easily constitute a massive data breach suggesting the mobile carriers had completely failed to protect the data of their respective users for the previous several years. It seems as if things, like security across the MNOs and across many other sectors has not developed and certainly has not

MAKING THE MATTER FAR WORSE (IOT AND 5G) 149

improved. Such a position is unreservedly unacceptable and a failing of all regulators.

Quantum computing is a new and exciting field that is at the intersection of mathematics, computer science, and physics. It concerns the utilisation of quantum mechanics to improve the efficiency of computation. Quantum computers perform calculations based on the probability of an object's state before it is measured, instead of just 1s and 0s which means they have the potential to process exponentially more data than today's classical computers. A single state, such as on or off or up and down or a 1 or 0, is called a bit. Quantum computing leverage quantum mechanical phenomena to manipulate information and to do this, quantum computers rely on quantum bits known as qubits. It is widely acknowledged and accepted that quantum computers will revolutionise the development and breakthroughs in science, medicines, machine learning, and materials to make more efficient devices and structures, financial strategies, and algorithms for the direction of critical services including emergencies. There is a huge, global movement and investments in quantum computing by virtually every government and major company. Suffice to say that investment in quantum capability is in the $billions, however, just like the first batch of PCs, security is clearly not an area that is even being considered...

In numerous discussions with quantum computing companies, and quantum companies on the fringe of quantum computing, it soon becomes apparent, that no one, literally no one is considering security and given the fact quantum computing is, and will be for the foreseeable future, utilising a hybrid of quantum and classical computing and therefore, will also be totally reliant on today's already heavily currently compromised PKI, certificates, and keys to share or forward any findings via any connected device, that takes us back to the weakest link in the chain, or the weakest security position.

The current landscape of corrupt Network Exploitation and PKI manipulation simply means that although quantum computing will create rapid and vastly improved computing capability, that data can be captured whilst in flight or even at rest from one device or organisation to another. Put simply, it will mean encryption and companies' data can be decrypted and breached more quickly. Also, data that was previously stolen in data breaches that was well encrypted will be easy to decrypt using quantum computing. This will include government data which is of course of great concern. Contrary to the verse by Matthew 5:5, it will not be the meek that inherit the earth, but those with quantum computers and who use them for nefarious purposes. Remind me, where are most quantum computers actually being manufactured? Today I have been sent an advert from a Chinese company offering a Quantum desktop computer for $5,000, clearly such an item will quickly become part of a cybercriminal's kit.

21
NSA OBSOLETE TLS PROTOCOLS

'It is difficult to get a person to understand something, when their salary depends on them not understanding it' Upton Sinclair 1934.

From 2015 onwards, Russia had clearly been successful in honing their cyber capabilities and had managed to fill their cyber arsenal. The arsenal store just happened to be filled with the very same methods and tools that the NSA and GCHQ had spent $billions on previously and many years to develop and perfect. They had gained the IP in a variety of ways, using a combination of Chinese style IP theft and simply bought the rest via organisations such as Shadow Brokers. The backdoors, once used exclusively for the NSA and GCHQ, were now available to everyone willing to pay and the Russians and Chinese were intent on having them and using them. The Russian attack on the Ukraine and then the DNC hack for over a year showed them as competent users and hackers of their newly found cyber weapons and they benefitted much in the same way the NSA and GCHQ had done and just like master magicians, by using misdirection and confusion to deceive, only this time it was with direct, nefarious intent and cyber espionage. Ukraine was a sitting duck with no defence as indeed was the DNC. The DNC did not have a single security professional in 2015 and 2016, that is only just several years ago leading up to the previous 2016 US elections. They had a set of disparate, insecure computers and connectivity to the internet. Undoubtedly and quite possibly, as much general surfing was taking place as putting important documents together. Insecure internet facing domains of the DNC resulted in what can be considered the catalyst that greatly influenced and determined the 2016 election results and outcome. The smear campaign whereby they stole emails from Hilary Clinton, embellished them, and splashed them all over social media. This destabilised the Clinton campaign by sowing seeds and questioning her integrity and

DOI: 10.1201/9781003204145-21

capability. As a gesture of outrage and disgust, Obama's government threw 35 Russian diplomats out of the country once details of Russia's meddling and infiltration was proven.

Shortly after the 2016 election, a full investigation took place by the FBI and the DNC. Although clearly, such an investigation would not alter the election outcome, no matter how shocked the world was. Donald Trump refused to accept the findings of Russian interference. It might be undermining his election victory. It was later proven and presented to Donald Trump by Clapper, Brennan, Comey, and Rogers along with supporting evidence of Putin's interference role. Soon thereafter Clapper and Brennan were dismissed. Comey went in front of Congress confirming Russia had intervened with the elections, and that he believed they would try to do so again, he was not wrong on both counts. He also confirmed that it was not exclusively a Republican or Democratic thing, they simply wanted to disrupt, and they were not particularly devoted to either party. Several months later, Trump met Putin, and obviously Putin's translator along with Trump's advisor, Rex Tillerson the Secretary of State. The meeting at a G20 summit in Germany lasted two and quarter hours and according to reports, Putin was directly posed the question three times on his involvement and influence in the 2016 elections, to which Putin answered, through his translator, there was none to each. Rex Tillerson was later fired on social media as opposed to in person some eight months later. It was acknowledged that the FBI and the DNC inaction coupled with a lacking security posture, allowed the Russian infiltration and data collection for months which proved to be incredibly costly and demonstrated, once again, the inability to provide, fit for purpose security. This situation is one we constantly encounter, from The Vatican to a major supplier of Her Majesty's government, even when evidence is shared, the inaction is nothing short of being complicit and in truth, could be considered a criminal act.

Over the last five years Russia, China, and other State Nations have honed and perfected their own cyberwarfare skills and effectively caught up, some could say they now have an advantage as defence has been a weak point for many years of our governments. This is mainly at the cost of the US and to a lesser extent, the UK, and others. State actors are literally running circles around the US and UK as they only need a single access point and security professionals must ensure comprehensive security across the entire business and in particular, all internet facing and connected security. However, that is where the failing is occurring. It is a well-known, industry fact that around 80% of all attacks are directed at the US and as Comey rightly said, the Russians will be back. The recent SolarWinds's attack is, I am afraid, the tip of the iceberg, it could have been one of many, similar organisations who all have inadequate security. If we were in the boxing world as my dear old recently departed friend and fighting partner Chalky would say; 'They've had so many rights they are begging for a left.' The sleight of hand and bombardment by our adversaries are ripping our countries, and our resolve apart. No one, including Bush or Obama, could have begun to even think or consider that the cyberwarfare and clandestine world domination of digital eavesdropping they sanctioned and commenced, would be turned 180 degrees back and used against everyone with such devastation. Was it just arrogance or simply foolishness? It is not easy to say, what we do know, is we are now fighting against all the odds and those charged with protecting us need to at least get visibility and know what they are protecting against and urgently. They also need to be given the tools to do the job properly before it is too late. The actions agencies and governments originally took are directly responsible for the insecure world we live in today and are unquestionably at a major crossroads. Do they finally come clean and share the intelligence and knowledge they have to assist the corporate world and governments to be able to do the basics and enable the world to at least keep their gloves up in the fight? Or do they continue using plausible deniability blaming the Russians, the Chinese, and the Iranians for their so-called 'sophisticated' attacks?

In an email exchange with Dr Ian Levy, the Technical Director of the NCSC, confirmed that invalid certificates on websites were of concern and that their webcheck system as well as their efforts since 2016 (coincidental timing to the DNC attacks, US elections, and others) was to inform companies of internet security. Here we are four years on, and it has clearly been a futile campaign and has clearly not worked well as our reports continually show and across numerous sectors including government themselves. Their program clearly lacks conviction, which is hardly surprising given the agencies' manipulation of TLS and SSL certificates to gain access themselves. Indeed, the redacted report I shared with Dr Ian Levy showed several expired certificates, and for several months, was as he personally said, of concern and if they were government domains, he would be asking questions. Why it was unchanged even after I confirmed it was an NCSC domain for some time, I simply cannot comment on. Several weeks later it remained unchanged and insecure, so much for Webchecker.

The darkened and grey world of espionage, from the cold war to today, is by its very nature fraught with danger and as has often been said, evidence is critical, so too is action. What our agencies have been guilty of is taking action that ultimately, completely undermined any chance of security and privacy, they weaponised the internet and made it totally unsafe. Furthermore, as was the case in the TalkTalk breach, they reinforced the fact that PKI was not of critical importance. Last year in the first six months of 2020, some 8 billion peoples' data was compromised, that is the equivalent of every man, woman, and child on the planet being compromised. It has been said many times by senior cyber government executives in the US that every US citizen should expect that their personal details will be compromised. Given our research and findings of the Korea DNS in Vote.gov, this should come as little surprise. They had access to hundreds of millions of PII data and all US citizens. The US government and agencies have for many years used third parties and paid twice as much due to the plethora of ex-service people covering their overheads and businesses. This has been a constant drain on budgets and increasing costs. One of the main benefits in addition to cash sloshing around, is Plausible Deniability, which is defined as:

> The ability of people, typically senior officials in a formal or informal chain of command, to deny knowledge of, or responsibility for any damnable actions committed by others in an organisational hierarchy because of the lack of evidence that can confirm their participation, even if they were personally involved in or at least wilfully ignorant of the actions.

Wow, we would all like that would we not especially if we wanted to take no responsibility for anything, ever. Responsibility should be viewed differently it could empower people by turning it around and giving everyone the ability to respond. If everyone takes no responsibility, who ultimately cares, so what?

The security sector urgently needs leadership and that is not earnt by having a title. It needs lots of it, not more yes people and excuses coupled to a culture of finger pointing and blame. Our digital world has received more than enough wake-up calls and cyberattacks to last a lifetime, and besides, how many does it take? Yet day after day, our governments and agencies are paying little more than lip service to defence at best. From the Department of Defence in Australia to the NCSC and the FBI, not one of them seem to want to drive change and start truly giving the advice and security that is urgently called for as can be evidenced by the plethora of breaches due to negligence. Their history and influence, at times, has been questionable and in many cases, counterproductive to assist anyone who is looking to be secure. There is a seemingly content position to witness travel companies, giant techs, foreign exchange, and government's technical and security companies get breached, call it a sophisticated attack, and blame the Russians or Chinese or someone else when in truth, it may have been a simple domain hijacking and PKI issue that could easily be averted. To date, not once have the US or Israel confessed to what the world knows was the part they played in the Stuxnet attack. Now the lessons learned from that, and other attacks have morphed into, and played out in the Sunburst attack. What is a near carbon copy attack and the use of digital certificates to carry their Sunburst malware ten years later. This includes a more than coincidental 13-day trigger and delay from infiltration to sending data back to the Mothership and four Zero Days. In the film Stuxnet, other US Agencies with the repurposing and development of Stuxnet were completely in the dark and thought they were being attacked themselves. It would prove not too long before they were by the Iranians using the same code that Stuxnet used against the US Banking sector. The disconnect is clear and vast between agencies and organisations and that includes internally. However, organisations are, incorrectly fed, and rely upon intelligence provided to them and are provided with false information, who questions the subjective, and bias opinion of them? This is one game that should cease with immediate effect before we lose to many more organisations or the economy driven down any further. We are in danger of heading to a Police State, however, with the way things are being allowed to happen, that State may not be managed by our own governments.

The average person may be computer literate, however, most even technically capable people, let alone Joe Public, do not understand domains, PKI, digital certificates, and encrypted keys. It is the main reason agencies created and manipulated PKI, TLS/SSL in the first place. In addition, very few can understand exactly what they were looking for, what to do if they found it, let alone how to address it. Yet our governments and agencies have seen and benefitted from the power and capabilities of Whitethorn® on several occasions and yet the agencies still want to dismiss it. They are afraid of its discovery capability and discovering the plethora of their own TLS and SSL plants they have in place. This would uncover their handywork that they have denied for years gaining intelligence and driving outcomes for years. That may have been okay before our adversaries had the same capability, but they have it now.

Take an average website, you type in the address, www.example.com and start navigating your way around the site. Did you notice the padlock on the address bar before the www? Was it there or was there Not Secure text? The reality is nowhere near enough people, including many in the security world fully understand the implications of a Not Secure domain. A secure website confirms the Authentication of the domain and company ownership, it ensures encryption of the data as well as the integrity of the data. A Not Secure domain confirms none of these. In essence, a Not Secure domain can be a Shadow website that can replicate or replace, taking the data by hijacking a website as was the case in 2018 BAWays.com and SolarWinds's breach in December 2020 to name just two. We have covered numerous examples throughout this book on companies that were breached whilst maintaining insecure, suboptimal internet facing sites. Everyone should ensure the website they use is correct and those developing and maintaining websites must ensure their visitors are secure to ensure compliance as well as privacy. By not doing so, it is a major reason digital theft and breaches are occurring with the frequency and scale we witness daily. The Agencies developed various programs with code names such as Quantum Insert to enable the redirection and catchment of internet traffic, so can adversaries. Be careful when surfing and companies have a responsibility to manage all domains to ensure they protect their clients.

According to Immuniweb today, 100% of mobile apps have at least two vulnerabilities, 97% of websites contain outdated software, 87%

NSA OBSOLETE TLS PROTOCOLS 157

of all airports have data leaks on public code repositories, 66% of airports have stolen credentials on the Dark Web. The Fortune 500 have 21 million credentials available on the Dark Web, 16 million were compromised over the last 12 months, 95% of stolen credentials are accessible in plain text. 85% of e-banking web applications failed GDPR tests, 49% of e-banking web applications failed PCI-DSS compliance tests, and 100% of the banks have security vulnerabilities or issues related to forgotten subdomains. Unquestionably we can consider this in many ways. One way is that there is much room for improvement of all these basic security areas, two, there is a huge pool of highly vulnerable organisations that can easily be breached. It becomes incredibly interesting why a prominent domain has only been scanned a handful of times such as the avsvmcloud.com used to breach SolarWinds, twice in the last year, but a SolarWinds's domain scanned hundreds of times. I am no Columbo, however if it was the company scanning and finding these incredible, numerous vulnerabilities, would, or even should, they be left. Through experience, our OSINT amalgamation enables us to second guess and almost predict forthcoming attacks or what might turn out to be a live attack due to the activity and overall vulnerability posture. If we spot it, chances are if and when a cybercriminal also spots the vulnerability, they will simply launch an attack whilst we are still trying to warn the organisation, heads-in-the-sand time.

Our campaigning over the last year on the importance of controlling and managing expired and deprecated Transport Layer Security (TLS) and Secure Socket Layer (SSL) certificates on websites, all domains, and subdomains, has finally made its mark and was acknowledged yesterday when the NSA, on the back of our efforts, launched their own information paper with the same advice. The NSA highlight the vulnerability and risk of sensitive data exposure and decryption. This marks a major shift by the NSA and hopefully, other agencies, including GCHQ, will adopt a similar position. This is urgently required. It is widely accepted that the agencies have manipulated TLS and SSL vulnerabilities to gain access over the last two decades. They have planted their own TSL/SSL certificates with administration privileges totally undetected and across a wide range of sectors, organisations, and countries. As I say, this NSA information paper marks a major shift in attitudes to their previous clandestine work they undertook and are by no means a coincidence of the work we have relentlessly driven. It doesn't mean they will stop; it just means they are in agreement and hopefully that will filter down to the guys at the coalface. This includes the SolarWinds's breach which, as we now know, gained initial access via a domain hijacking which was due to an obsolete and invalid TLS/SSL certificate on an insecure subdomain. The certificate was supposed to be ensuring security, however, due to negligence, created a completely insecure position. What was supposed to provide strength and security enforced weakness and insecurity.

Knowing what to do and not doing what one knows is often the reason for such issues in the first place, however it is a great start and throughout this book I have been forthright on errors made, however on this, I applaud the NSA and would be delighted to work with them and GCHQ to drive this urgently required message. As we witness, even when NIST provides papers and advice, it is rarely followed through. False information, inaction, and negligence are the main reasons for the issues we face daily.

The world's population, not just the governments and agencies, need to decide and act. That decision can be to carry on ignoring what we know, or certainly should know, and that is by ignoring basic internet facing and connected security it makes everyone an easy target and one by one (or multiples in the case of Blackbaud, SolarWinds, and others) we will all lose out to breach after breach, and witness our global economy continue sliding into the red. Internet security and digital certificates were created to provide digital communication, privacy and security, we must decide to enforce and reinforce this position with diligence. However, until that happens, we will witness losses continuing to ramp up to this year's figure of $16 billion losses and costs a day, every day, and counting. The world has truly gone crazy, and far too much power and influence has been given to the few, and those few have made, and continue to make, far too many mistakes. Everyone must demand security at source, including the executives that have been incorrectly swayed and chosen to ignore evidence to date. Our democracy and survival are dependent upon it. Or, we can of course be inactive, ignore the evidence, and wait for things to simply get worse.

We are all around for, and have a limited time, however we also have dependants, children, and grandchildren. What and who has

NSA OBSOLETE TLS PROTOCOLS

gone before are in effect responsible for the chaos we witness today along with the added heartache of being breached. They can draw their pensions and live a privileged life. The legacy they have left however will affect their, and our children and grandchildren. It is this human instinct that we must capture that can and will unite us. Insecurity has become a global pandemic, there is a vaccine for it, and we have the formula, everyone has the formula but must be willing to use and adopt it. We must prioritise and address security, not consider it sometime later. The challenges and simply vulgar situation that has divided nations, created disconnect between religions and faiths, and is driving our world into a worsening case of 'Haves and Have Nots' like never witnessed before. Will see the haves being criminals and terrorists and is clearly not a future anyone wants or could look forward to and yet, that is exactly what is being allowed to happen, day after day and by our very own governments.

Picture the scene where the tumble weed blows down 5th Avenue or Pall Mall or across London Bridge due to the economic collapse and cybercrime and you will get the picture. No one wants any digital device for fear of them turning against them, sharing their location, data, and stripping them of any personal information and funds. That is the future we are all currently signed up for if we continue to do nothing to address and correct it, and that means agencies working with, not against private security organisations with ensuring basic security is the global congruent message.

The definition of insanity is constantly doing the same thing over and over and expecting a different result. This is exactly what is happening in the world of security today. There is much talk of innovation. AI, Quantum Computing, Autonomous vehicles, and Smart Cities among the discussions and yet, no one is willing, apart from us that is, to innovate PKI. This area has been abused and manipulated for over 20 years by governments and their agencies to provide full digital and backdoor access, and that access, the methods, and the techniques, are now used on ever increasing scales and frequency by our adversaries. As Colin Powell said, 'If it ain't broke, don't fix it' is the slogan of the complacent, the arrogant or the scared. It's an excuse for inaction, a call to non-arms.' You must decide which applies to our governments and agencies.

22

WHAT DOES THE FUTURE HOLD? BY ASKING BETTER QUESTIONS, WE WILL GET BETTER ANSWERS AND TAKE BETTER ACTION

The better the questions, the better the answers.

As the SolarWinds's breach continues to roll on, continuing to gain momentum, and thousands of casualties, more companies are hardly surprisingly starting to consider their third-party supply chains and the additional vulnerabilities these may pose on an ongoing basis. It is always a shame when catastrophes act as a catalyst, however often this is the case. There are indeed many lessons to be learned from this breach, not least of all liability. Having said that, you should certainly not be throwing stones if you live in a glasshouse, which sadly is in most cases as our research continually shows right through to government.

The challenge, and this is a monumental one, is not about security, but getting people to act and ensure security as fit for purpose and that simply include lessons learned from previous breaches. Take the RSA breach in 2011. In March 2011, Art Coviello revealed a doozie of a cyberattack on the company whereby hackers had broken into RSA's servers (internet facing of course) and stole information about their SecurID two-factor authentication products. The attack utilised a phishing recruitment campaign and social engineering to gain PII data and access. They also used Poison Ivy RAT as a trojan to gain remote control access. Then there was the major breach at Juniper Networks a few years later that revealed a security breach that enabled the modification of Juniper's software, software that was already using an NSA-designed algorithm which had long been suspected of containing a backdoor. The same year Russia managed to infiltrate

DOI: 10.1201/9781003204145-22

161

162   **STUXNET TO SUNBURST**

the DNC and for over a year manipulated and exfiltrated data which, along with social engineering and smear campaigns, greatly influenced the 2016 US election outcome.

But seriously, what lessons were learned and what improvements have been made? The sad answer is very few lessons and very few improvements. The companies and governments named throughout this book and above, still maintain insecure positions facing, and connected to the internet. As my dear old friend from IBM just said to me on the phone, 'who would want to be a CISO and juggle the budgets, which will always never be big enough.' The truth is as I said, this is not solely about budgets, it is about action, knowledge, and prioritising. An example of this is SolarWinds. What budget and focus does this cybersecurity firm have on their own security? We would all guess substantial right? Yet a single digital certificate enabled a subdomain to become invalid and allow a domain hijacking resulting in what is being touted as a $1 trillion cost/loss. It is not that they did not want to spend or renew a cert, they simply did not have control or management and as such, their entire security, and that of their clients, was worthless. It was undermined and attacked in most cases.

This week alone we shared two major insecure government situations with the NCSC. The first being an insecure Number 10 domain with hundreds of associated and linked domains being made insecure and the Intelligence and Security Committee of Parliament, who is also blatantly maintaining a Not Secure domain and via the links, putting the entire ecosystem in a vulnerable position. This is not a simple error; this is nothing short of gross negligence and presents a real and present danger to National Security. As a footnote to this and the sharing of intelligence with the NCSC, we have offered to work with the government to provide a full audit of all.gov domains and remediate as required, it is clearly obvious that many are not secure as we have demonstrated and as Dr Ian Levy (Technical Director NCSC) said: 'The certificate is actually misconfigured on the CDN node. The TLS 1.0 support is poor! So without for a second saying this is acceptable for a government, site, what vulnerability do you believe this attract?... It is worth adding one final time, by being Not Secure, a website cannot be authenticated, the data lacks integrity and can be altered and the data is maintained in plain text as opposed to cipher text (encrypted). The domain, or the domain owner, in this

WHAT DOES THE FUTURE HOLD?   **163**

case the UK government, is also falling foul of their own UKDPS and GDPR. Privacy laws as an IP address constitutes PII and as such, a Not Secure website falls foul of providing security or privacy for a casual user let alone a client or member of the company.

My response was, in the current climate any such exposure in Her Majesty's Government (HMG), and, No. 10 should be seen as unacceptable. Such vulnerabilities need to be considered in the bigger picture of adverse opportunities. I went on, it was in this week that we also discovered that the Intelligence and Security Committee (ISE) is also maintaining a Not Secure site which makes a mockery of the entire intelligence fraternity and clearly demonstrates inadequate controls and management across HMG. These are not one-off issues; they are systemic issues.

Please do not get me wrong, we appreciate that the size of the challenge is vast because the monster has been allowed, even encouraged to grow to such a size, however it is often reliant upon people to address the issues that may not realise the critical importance of ensuring internet facing security as well as PKI, let alone understanding it. The NCSC and GCHQ must adapt to the challenges of these APTs that utilise these vulnerabilities as in the SolarWinds's infiltration via an insecure and unmanaged subdomain before there are no companies left to protect. My emails concluded by saying; Just a thought, why don't we conduct a full audit of all.gov related sites to enable better controls and management? It could prove most beneficial. I am yet to receive a reply. I am however tempted to undertake such research and share it.

The point to all the above is clear, the UK government, their agencies, and their counterparts are simply not addressing internet security anywhere near enough and immaterial if it was lessons learned from Project Aurora, Stuxnet, Not Petya, or even SolarWinds, time after time the lack of digital certificate management and controls has created the world's most devastating attacks. The evidence is unequivocal, and that is this area. Even the biggest tech giants and governments today have woefully and inadequately managed and happily manipulated internet facing security and PKI controls.

Given this situation, companies calling for third-party security audits are doing little more than paying even more lip service to a fashion, a trend that is possibly considering short-term profits and

164 STUXNET TO SUNBURST

ongoing liabilities more than ensuring security, which may, in the event of a breach, prove their continued insecure positions was and has been, self-inflicted. I have read reports over this last week of senior security experts claiming they will not work with third parties until they show, via a pen test they are secure. All the while, the company making such demands are insecure themselves, and with numerous, internet facing security issues. Think of this like a Covid-19 test once a year, you cannot guarantee you are not carrying or will not catch the virus the other 364 days that year. Without ongoing controls and management, the result can, and will be, bias for that day. It is like passing a driving test or a regulatory test, it does not mean you are a good driver or have ongoing compliance, it simply means you just passed. We know of many organisations that are all too pleased to 'assist' in such cases. Indeed, CBEST last year was held accountable for producing papers to provide compliance for their clients, so much so that it was a given...

The digital world along with the government and agencies are at a major crossroads right now and discussions going on in the Situations Rooms around the world are possibly not asking the right questions. The questions that are currently being asked are was the attack an act of cyberwar, terrorism, or vandalism, and what is the appropriate and proportional response, if any? As Paul Nakasone, the Director of United States National Security Agency said; 'Our adversaries do not fear us.' So being bigger, better funded, having more resources and more methods and tools for Network Exploitation, and PKI manipulation has not had the desired effect. We have seen spending over the last two decades on cybersecurity go from tens of $millions to hundreds of $billions, and losses go from hundreds of $millions to $trillions in the same time frame. We have also witnessed tens of thousands of resources across the globe focused on cyber and yet we are losing and losing on a massive scale. The SolarWinds's breach alone is already, within weeks, is as I mentioned, predicted to surpass $1 trillion in costs and losses and we have barely started the year.

The question the teams in these Situation Rooms, and others like it, have failed to ask: How can we ensure and assure all companies and governments have the discipline to ensure basic security facing the internet and online on an ongoing basis? Think about that simple question for just a minute. You can have the best teams, firewalls,

WHAT DOES THE FUTURE HOLD? 165

encryption, antivirus software, and so on, just like SolarWinds, governments, and thousands of other corporates and yet a single digital certificate for a domain, or as in case after case throughout this book, internally, and it can facilitate and enable initial infiltration and allow the enemy within your enterprise and frequently, totally undetected as was the case of the hijacked domain that enabled the massive Sunburst attack. Real security connecting you to the internet would greatly reduce being targeted, successful attacks and breaches. This is where proper investment is lacking and although some areas are being covered. Take www.clemson.edu, for example. $111 million was awarded to this university to teach cybersecurity to the US manufacturing sector and yet Clemson university has a totally Not Secure, highly vulnerable homepage. What lessons will they be teaching and providing? It is sheer negligence and should be withdrawn. We are witnessing the rewarding of insecurity and incompetence and hoping they just teach better than their own poor and inadequate standards.

We believe the question every government should be asking is, if we reset PKI in the full knowledge, we, as agencies around the world have manipulated it and we all, including our adversaries, have the same capability, should we not start focusing on defensive security capability as opposed to continuing to bang the drum and spending $billions upon $billions on offensive capability? It has not dissuaded anyone, and the attacks keep coming, more frequently and on larger scales. Many Directors and government officials will testify to the fact that the Chinese and Russians are already within their CNI, but because they continue to ignore gaining visibility by using incomplete and fractional PKI capability, those vulnerabilities remain undetected and ready to be primed and released. How can a small company like ours identify and share details with the US government of a Korean DNS within the US Central Voting system that they were totally unaware of? The reason is their focus is not on security, it is, as they have been found guilty of, focusing on offensive capabilities and at a massive cost. The balance is completely incorrect.

There is a huge amount of intelligent people and leaders, however why they are so hell bent in acting foolishly and acting like lesser intelligent people seeking revenge and wanting their adversaries to accept defeat without a fight is quite simply bizarre. In the Nuclear age the threat was matched and if an advantage was being sought, it

166 STUXNET TO SUNBURST

was quite quickly nullified. In today's cyberwar age, threat actors do not need massive budgets and resources in their thousands, they need some bright young guns with a keyboard and an access point. That access point, along with something that resembles the wild west so far as digital certificates are concerned, enable a small team to launch attacks on CNIs, governments, Financial Services companies, or SolarWinds from thousands of miles away and short, just short of being party to the breach to occurring, complacency and negligence unequivocally let the attack commence, and continue. I would go so far as to say the attack was initially identified as part of an overall reconnaissance program and SolarWinds, and many others, identified as possible targets due to their insecure position. Many more such attacks are currently in flight and in different stages, organisations simply do not know, yet. It could have been any organisation in the chain, it may well be many others that are in the throes of such attacks but are totally unaware. Such a program can identify targets that are vulnerable and simply line them up. This will not stop, slow down, or reduce in magnitude. SolarWinds may mark the beginning of a new era of cyberattacks, however it has been coming for the last several years. There will be many more and many in flight right now...

We have gone from Project Aurora and the use of digital code to cause collateral damage, Stuxnet the world's first digital weapon, and now Sunburst in the space of 15 years. What was used to ensure security, is being used against us to identify our own insecurities, history is clear and the outcome catastrophic, the question is what next?

This book develops day after day as attacks become better dissected and understood. Our job is to drive security, security knowledge, and the adoption of good basic security not just writing about the history of security and its manipulation and exploitation, originally by the agencies and governments, and now by criminals. Let me leave you with this thought, there is just under 8 billion people in the world. If just 1,000 of that population wanted to attack the remaining 7 billion plus continually digitally, in today's current insecure state, the 1,000 will win...

Zero Trust requires Zero Trust Architecture and Authentication, until PKI is robust, fit for purpose and delivers upon that, not just pay lip service hiding backdoors, Digital Trust in any form is like a cheap and nasty broken watch, it will never work.

WHAT DOES THE FUTURE HOLD?

Building any Operating System (OS), Cloud, Network, Quantum Computers, Autonomous Vehicles, or Smart Cities without PKI controls, management, and authentication on an ongoing basis, will just lead to larger and more frequent devastating cyberattacks, collateral damage, and the loss of human life.

Index

A

Abbasi, Fereydoon, 23
Abbott, Tony, 91–93
Accenture, 55
AC Dayton Cobra, 37
Actionable Intelligence, 72, 79
act of war, 20, 57
Adleman, Leonard, 2
Advanced Network Technology
     (ANT), 122, 123
Afghanistan, 8
Ahmadinejad, Mahmoud, 23
AI, 18, 90, 135, 159
AIG, 28
Air France Flight 4590, 41
Air Gapped, 22
Airlines, 78
airports, 8, 157
Alan Touring, 30
Alaska, 94, 95
Allies information, 10, 11
Allies Israel, 20
Allsopp, Connor, 147
American Airlines flights, 7

American Federation of Government
     Employees, 46
American Intelligence, 30
Americold, 134
Andretti, Mario, 38
Apax Partners, 60
Appelbaum, Jacob, 122
Apple, 2
Arak, 20
Archer, 79, 132–134
Archuleta, Katherine, 46
Armco, 39, 135
Artex, 47
Association of British Insurers
     (ABI), 56–58
Aston Martin Championship, 37–39
Aston race car, 40
Astra Zeneca, 131, 133
attack victims, 115, 116
Audit, 31, 33
Aurora project, *see* Project Aurora
Australia, 91–97
Australian Defence, 92, 94, 108
Australian Signals Directorate, 13
authentication, 2, 5, 79, 85, 125, 156

169

170 INDEX

Autonomous vehicles, 65, 159, 167
Autosport, 37
Avengers superheroes, 46

B

Bakker, Anthony, 99
Bamford, James, 9
Banking Executives, 27
Barclays Bank, 72
Belgacom, 123
Belkin, 117
Besley, Tim, 130
Biden, Joe, 117, 119
Big 4, 25, 31–34, 71
Big Bang system, 45
Big Brother, 9
Blackbaud, 99–103, 123, 158
BlackEnergy, 106, 107
BLARNEY, 122
Bloomberg, 113
Bombe, 30
Bossert, Thomas P., 115
Boston security company, 148
Bowie, David, 28
Bradley Smith of Microsoft, 112
Brands Hatch, 38
Breach Fatigue, 77
Brennan, 152
Britain's Government
    Communications
    Headquarters (GCHQ), 13
British GT Championship, 38
British Intelligence, 30
Bro, 123
Brock, Peter, 37
BT, 146
Bundesnachrichtendienst
    (Germany), 13
Bush, George W, 8, 9, 20, 21, 53,
    126, 153

C

California, 7
Cambridge University, 131
Camerfirma, 101
Cameron, David, 29, 147
Canada Pension Plan Investment
    Board (CPP
    Investments), 113
Canada's Community Security
    Establishment, 13
Cardiff University, 79
Catholic News Agency, 87
CBEST, 164
Centurion, 60
certificate
    Chinese Internet Network
        Information Centre
        (CNNIC) certificates,
        101–103
    digital certificates, 2–4, 6, 22–24,
        50, 54–55, 81, 88, 137, 141,
        155, 158
    Ericson obsolete certificate, 145
    FLYING PIG SSL certificate, 33
    Microsoft digital certificates, 22
    PGP certificate, 138
    root certificate, 4, 5
    Secure Socket Layer (SSL)
        certificate, 5, 24, 25, 29–31,
        33, 34, 47, 51, 73, 83, 93,
        101, 126, 131, 138, 140, 141,
        153, 156–158
    self-signing certificates, 112
    SolarWinds digital certificates, 6
    SSH certificate, 138
    standard digital certificate, 4
    Transport Layer Security (TLS)
        certificate, 5, 24, 25, 29–31,
        33, 34, 51, 61, 73, 80, 93,
        101, 123, 126, 131, 138, 140,
        141, 153, 157, 158

INDEX

certificate authorities (CAs), 2–4, 70, 102, 103, 141
certificate lifecycle management (CLM) market, 34
Chalky, 153
Chaos Communications Congress in Hamburg, 122
Chatham House rules, 65
Cheltenham, 29, 47
China, 46, 49, 93, 105, 107, 110, 129, 132, 152
Chinese Intelligence cyberattack, 45
Chinese Internet Network Information Centre (CNNIC) certificates, 101–103
Chinese State actors, 54
CIA, 8, 10, 11, 19, 20, 24, 95, 107
Cigarettes, 90
CIO, 32–33, 66, 70, 145
CIP, 71
ciphertext, 83
Cisco Systems, 117
CISO, 69–70, 72, 101, 162
clandestine manipulation, 25
Clapper, 152
Class Action lawsuits, 50, 76, 110
Class Actions, 56, 58, 89
Clemson University, 80, 165
Clinton, Bill, 121, 126
Clinton, Hilary, 151
Cloud, 103, 167
Cloudflare, 18, 110
Club House, 7
Cocks, Clifford, 3
code name, 10, 15, 29, 122, 138
Comey, 152–153
command and control (C2), 6, 16, 24, 42, 55, 71, 86, 103, 106, 109, 122, 144
Commissioner of Nuclear Power, 16

Common Vulnerabilities and Exposures (CVEs), 16, 32, 47, 51, 78, 94, 95
Community Security Establishment (Canada), 13
Computer Misuse Act (CMA), 62, 88
Computer Network Exploitation (CNE), 9, 73, 93, 140
Computer Network Operations, 121, 122
computers, *see* personal computers (PCs)
computer security issues, 107
Concorde flight, 41
Congress, 19, 115, 152
Content Delivery Network (CDN), 24, 55, 70, 103, 110, 162
continental flight, 41
contractor market, 19
conversion, 21
coronavirus, 129–135
counterintelligence, 45
Covid-19, 16, 66, 69, 79, 87, 89, 97, 127
    breaches, 129–135
    testing company, 89
    testing programme, 147
    vaccine, 133–134
Coviello, Art, 161
Cozy Bear/Fancy Bear, 107
Critical National Infrastructure (CNI), 15, 25, 34, 65, 67, 109
    CNI Board, 71
    organisation, 25, 55, 65–67, 69–71, 73, 140
Crowdstrike, 118
Crypto AG, 10, 11, 24, 142
cryptographic digital keys, 2
cryptography, 2–3, 34, 88
Crypto mining, 79

172   **INDEX**

CSA, 84
Customer Proprietary Network
    Information (CPNI), 148
cyberattackers, 47, 62, 75–81, 86, 93
cyberattacks, 5, 14, 17, 20, 23, 25, 29,
    43, 45, 49, 73, 91, 94, 106,
    107, 110, 127, 141
Cyber Audits, 33
cyber breaches, 105
cybercrime, 43, 79, 140
cybercriminals, 5, 17, 24, 25, 42,
    60–63, 81, 85–87, 92, 126,
    134–135
Cyber Defence Agencies, 92, 93
Cybereason, 148
cyber espionage, 49, 151
Cyber Geneva Convention, 14
Cyber Insurance, 33, 56–58, 101
Cyber intelligence, 14, 126
cyber nuisance, 14
cyber offensive capability, 14
cyber providers, 112
cybersecurity, 70, 71, 80, 117, 162
Cybersecurity and Infrastructure
    Security Agency (CISA),
    114, 115
    updated guidance, 118
cyberspace, 19
cyberterrorism, 14, 49
cyber vandalism, 14, 49
cyberwar, 14, 25, 80, 105, 109
cyberwarfare, 8, 29, 112

D

DanderSpritz software, 125
Dark Web, 4, 34, 77, 106, 157
data flow, 50
data gathering, 9
data harvesting, 84
data integrity, 79, 84
Davos, 29
decryption, 30

Defence domains, 97
Defence Intelligence Headquarters
    (Japan), 13
Delaware, 95, 140
Deloitte, 116, 117
DELVE, 130
Democratic National Committee
    (DNC), 107–109, 125, 131,
    151, 152, 162
Denial-of-Service attack, 106
Department of Homeland Security
    (DHS), 17, 28, 115
    supply chain, 62
Department of US Treasury, 27
Der Spiegel article, 122
Deterrence Theory, 121, 126, 142
Dictator, 49
Diffie, Whitfield, 2
Diffie Hellman key exchange, 2
Digicert, 3, 70
digital certificates, 2–4, 6, 22–24, 50,
    54–55, 81, 88, 137, 141, 155,
    158; *see also* certificate
digital code, 19, 42, 111, 126, 166
digital communications, 9–11, 158
digital cyber intelligence, 19
digital doorbells, 143
digital eavesdrop, 122
digital eavesdropping, 3, 11
Digital Forensics, 88
digital ID theft, 83
digital machines, 3
Digital Sense, 116
Digital Trust, 4–6, 14, 50, 77, 81, 166
Digital Warfare, 42
Digital Weapon, 23, 42
Director for National
    Intelligence, 108
DOD supply chain, 17, 28, 62, 97,
    109, 110, 137
Domain Admin Access, 81, 92, 112
Domain ecosystems, 84
Domain hijacking, 18, 47

INDEX

Domain Name System (DNS), 24, 70, 94, 110
  partner, 18
  provider, 55, 103
Domenillo, Victor, 92, 93
Double Hatter, 67
DoublePulsar backdoor, 124
Doughnut building, 29
D'Souza, Tony, 61
Duqu, 23, 105, 120

E

Easter Eggs, 32
easyJet, 75–77
Edinburgh University, 79
elections, 10, 78, 94–95, 107, 151
Ellis, James, 3
Elnahal, Shereef, 85, 135
Emergency Services, 145, 146
emergency workers, 8
encryption, 2, 30, 79, 84
Enigma machine, 2, 30
EPCC systems, 132
The Equation Group, 124
Equation Group Cyber Weapons Auction, 124
Equifax breach, 49–50
Ericson obsolete certificate, 145
EternalBlue, 120, 124
European Medicines Agency (EMA), 134
Evans, Mark, 145, 146
EV CA, 102
Everything Everywhere, 146

F

F1 drivers, 37, 38
Facebook, 10
FAIRVIEW, 122
fake sites, 84
Fancy Bear attacks, 107

Fannie Mae, 27, 28
FBI, 8, 33, 94–95, 110, 115–116, 137, 152
Federal Agent, 109
Federal Communications Commission (FCC), 53
Federal Reserve, 27
FINABLR, 60–62
financial collapse of 2008, 57
financial ruin, 56
Financial Services industry, 60
Financial Times, 109
FireEye, 87, 103, 107, 113, 114, 138
FISMA, 115
Five Eyes, 13, 93, 122
5G, 145
Flame, 23, 120
Flight 4590, 41
FLYING PIGS, 24, 29–31, 33
Foreign and Commonwealth affairs, 29
Forensics, 31, 33, 46
Formula race, 40
Forte Mead, 47
Fortune 500, 62, 157
Fox, David J., 46
FOXACID, 122
Freddie Mac, 27, 28
Further Education (FE), 131

G

G20 summit, 107, 152
Gauntlet, 43
GDPR regulations, 4, 58, 76, 79, 89, 146, 162
Germany, 66, 122, 152
  Bundesnachrichtendienst, 13
GitHub repository, 124
Global Fintech Holding AG (GFIH), 62
Gold Standard laptop, 32, 67, 101, 102

INDEX

Google, 5, 83, 101, 102, 109, 110
Google Chrome, 83
Gopinath, Gita, 130
government agencies, 112, 140–142
Government Communications
    Headquarters (GCHQ), 3,
    10, 13, 24, 29, 30, 33, 55, 67,
    72, 73, 109, 123, 126, 140,
    144, 151, 157, 158, 163
Government Security Bureau
    (New Zealand), 13
Grand Prix circuit, 38
Great Depression, 27, 130

H

Haji-Ioannou, Sir Stelios, 76
Hamilton, Duncan, 38
Hanley, Matthew, 147
Hannigan, Robert, 109, 144
Harding, Dido, 147
Hawkins, Adrian, 108, 109, 131
Hawkins DNC, 109
Hayden, Michael, 23
Health and Education sectors, 130
Health and Health Insurance
    sectors, 78
Healthcare centre, 135
Healthcare sector, 85
Health Centres, 78
Health Insurance, 78
Health Warning message, 90
HEARTBEAT, 24
Hellman, Martin, 2
Herbert, Johnny, 38
Heritage Racing, 38
Her Majesty's Government
    (HMG), 163
Hill, Graham, 37
Hiscox, 88
Homeland Security Department, 46,
    108, 126
Hotel Chain, 53

House of Representatives, 9
HTTP sites, 17, 83, 89, 122, 134
HTTPS protocol, 17, 83–85, 110
Hubble Road, 29
Hunt, James, 38
HUSH PUPPY, 24, 29–31
hydroxychloroquine, 133
Hypertext Transfer Protocol
    (HTTP) sites, 83

I

IBM, 1, 125, 162
Idaho laboratory, 14
Immuniweb, 156
Imperva, 55, 70
incompetence, 80, 84, 91, 100, 121,
    132, 165
Industrial Control Systems (ICS),
    15, 42
Information Commissioner Office
    (ICO), 55, 78, 147
Innes Ireland Trophy, 37
Institute of Economic Affairs
    (IEA), 133
Insurance companies, 56
Insured, 57
Insurer, 57, 58
Intel, 117
Intelligence agencies, 9, 107, 112
Intelligence and Security Committee
    (ISE), 162, 163
intelligence committees, 9
Intelligence community, 13, 94, 107
International Atomic Energy Agency
    (IAEA), 20, 111
International Monetary Fund
    (IMF), 130
Internet of things (IoT) devices, 1,
    143–144
internet security, 18, 158
The Interview, 49
investigation request, 115

INDEX

175

IPO, 60, 61, 84
Iran, 20, 111
Iranian Nuclear Power, 15, 21, 23,
    42, 111
Iranian Nuclear Programme, 21
Iranian Nuclear Scientists, 23
Irish Education Governing body, 143
ISPs, 83
Israel, 20
Israeli 8220 cyber force, 21
ITPS, 116
Ivy League Universities, 80

J

Japan's Defence Intelligence
    Headquarters, 13
Jobs, Steve, 2, 78
Johnson, Boris, 119
Juniper Networks, 161

K

Kaspersky Labs, 124
Kennedy, John F., 105
Key Bridge Marriott, 53
KeyPoint, 45
KillDisk malware, 106
Killer, 69
Killer Rat, 55
killswitch, 115
Kim Jong-un, 49
Korean DNS, 33–34, 94–95, 154

L

Laden, Osama Bin, 8, 19
legal privacy laws, 58
legal team, 33, 81
Lehman Brothers, 28
Le Mans, 38, 39
Lets Encrypt, 3, 131

Levy, Ian, 137–140, 153, 162
LinkedIn, 78, 88, 137, 140
Liska, Allan, 117
Little Green Men, 106
London Bridge, 159
London School of Economics
    (LSE), 61, 79, 131
London Stock Exchange, 60
Lorenz machine, 2, 30

M

M&A, 101
machine
    digital, 3
    Enigma, 2
    Lorenz, 2
    scanning machines, 8
malicious activity, 91
Malware, 6, 23, 61, 77, 81
Malwarebytes, 51
Man-in-the-Middle attacks, 5,
    47, 102
Marriott, Bill, 53–54, 66
Marriott, J. Willard, 53
Marriott International, 53–58
Marriott World Trade Centre
    Hotel, 53
Martin, Ciaran, 56
Martin, Harold, 125
mass intelligence gathering, 11
Maze Ransomware organisations, 18,
    94, 110
McQueen, Steve, 39, 40
MCS holdings test network, 102
media coverage, 114
MI5, 11, 137
microcomputer, 1
Microsoft, 5, 101, 109, 112, 114, 116,
    118, 124, 143
    digital certificates, 22
    investigation, 116
    vulnerabilities, 30

INDEX

Middle East respiratory Syndrome (MERS), 129
Ministry of Defence (MOD), 23, 65–67, 73, 97, 109
Missile manufactures, 78
Mnuchin, Steven, 117
Mobile Network Operator (MNO) market, 146–148
Moderna, 133
Modus Operandi, 28, 112
monopolies, 20
Monster, 48, 126
Morrison, Scott, 91–93
Mortgage-Backed Securities (MBS), 27, 57
Mothership, 33, 101, 155
Motor Racing, 38
Moyer, Chris, 144
Mozilla, 5, 83, 101
Muncher, 38, 39
Munich Security conference, 29
MyServiceNSW data, 92

N

Nakasone, Paul, 112, 164
NASA, 17, 88
Natanz, 15, 20, 22, 23, 111
National Cyber Security program, 29
National Grid, 15, 16
National Institutes of Health, 115
National Intelligence Estimate (NIE), 20
National Nuclear Security Administration, 116
National Security, 69, 70, 72, 137, 140, 162
National Security Agency (NSA), 8, 10, 11, 13, 20, 21, 24, 29, 30, 33, 90, 95, 118, 121–124, 126, 140, 151, 158, 161
NSA Obsolete Transport Layer Security (TLS) Protocols, 151–159

National Security Council (NSC), 114
Nation State, 28, 42, 46, 48, 57, 69
NATO, 29, 34
    client, 126
    installation, 34
NCSC, 50–51, 56, 75, 76, 93, 137, 140, 154, 162, 163
Netanyahu, Benjamin, 20
Netanyahu's Unit 8200, 20
Netdecisions, 116
Netscape, 3
Network, 126, 167
Network Exploitation, 9, 22, 29, 48, 73, 126, 144, 149, 164
Newark, 41
New York Times, 86, 142
New Zealand's Government Security Bureau, 13
9/11
    and the creation of mass data collection in the name of security, 7–11
    terrorist attacks of, 19, 53, 142
NIST drives, 31, 158
Northeast blackout, 15
North Koreas missile program, 49
NotPetya, 57, 163
Not Secure domain, 5, 17–18, 47, 57, 60–62, 75, 77, 79–81, 83–90, 92, 100, 101, 110, 131–133, 135, 148, 156, 162, 163
Nuclear, 67, 69, 73
Nuclear capability, 70
Nuclear Energy Company, 90
Nuclear Power sites, 20
Nuclear Programme, 28
Nuclear Rat, 55
Nuclear space, 105
nuclear warheads, 20
nuclear weapon programme, 20
Nuclear Weapons, 121
Nvidia, 117

INDEX

O

O2 PKI team, 145
O2 Telefonica, 145
OAKSTAR, 122
Obama, Barak, 49, 107, 126, 153
Obsolete TLS protocols
management, 141
OEM Certificate chains, 32
OFCOMS, 147
offensive capability, 14, 15
Office of Inspector General, 47–48
Office of Personnel Management
(OPM), 14, 45–51
Olympic Games, 19–21, 23, 103,
124, 126
Omnisec, 11, 24, 142
OPEC (organisation of Petroleum
exporting countries), 123
Open-Source Intelligence (OSINT),
18, 87, 89
amalgamation, 157
capabilities, 61, 90
research, 93, 94
technology, 62, 96
Operating System (OS), 167
OPM, 46, 54
Orange, 146
Oulton Park Gold Cup, 37
out-of-control race car, 42
Outsourced IT, 55
Oxford University, 79, 131,
133–134
Ozment, Andy, 46, 107

P

Padlock, 17
Paedophiles, 143
Pall Mall, 159
Pandora, 24
Pastebin, 124
PEDDLECHEAP payload, 125
Penetration Team, 33

Penrose, John, 147
Pentagon, 8
The Perfect Weapon (David
Sanger), 107
Permanent Record (Edward
Snowden), 31
personal computers (PCs), 1–6, 126,
143, 144
Personal Identifiable Information
(PII) data, 49
Personal Protective Equipment
(PPE), 133
Petya cyberattack (2017), 124
Pfizer, 133
PGP certificate, 34, 138
PII data, 45, 54, 58, 75, 76, 78, 83, 86,
89, 92, 99, 131, 146–148,
154, 161
Pilgrims Drop, 38, 39
PKI, 16, 18, 22–24, 31–35, 40–41, 43,
48, 50, 55, 80, 86, 97,
101–103, 123, 126, 135,
137, 140, 141, 145, 146, 149,
154, 155, 159, 163–167
Planet Scale change, 83
Plausible Deniability, 10, 13, 19, 50,
140, 143, 154
Poison Ivy RAT, 161
Pompeo, Mike, 117
Powell, Colin, 159
Power Stations, 73
President's Surveillance Program, 9
PRISM, 9, 13, 29
Privacy and Electronic
Communications
Regulations, 146
Programmable Logic Controller
(PLC), 21, 42
Project Aurora, 14–16, 19–21, 39, 42,
105, 111, 163, 166
Project Manager, 67
Proof of Concept (PoC), 66, 67, 70
property prices in 2006, 27
Public, Joe, 126, 141, 156

178　　　　INDEX

Public Key Infrastructure (PKI), 2–6,
  65, 66, 69, 71, 73
Pulse Secure, 61
Putin, Vladimir, 107, 152
PWC, 61

Q

al-Qaeda terrorists, 7–8
Quantum Computers, 150, 167
Quantum Computing, 135, 149, 159
QUANTUM INSERT (QI), 24, 29,
  123, 156
QUANTUMSQUIRREL, 122
Query Focused Dataset (QFD), 30

R

race cars, development of, 38
racing drivers, 38
Raisers Edge, 99
Ramada International Hotels, 53
Ramakrishna, Sudhakar, 113
Ransomware, 17, 34, 42, 60, 61, 77,
  85, 86, 110, 135
Remote Access Trojans (RATs),
  55, 69
Republican National Committee
  (RNC), 107
Respiratory etiquette, 129
Reuters, 112
Risk Management, 37
Rivest, Ron, 2
Rogers, 152
Root Cause Analysis (RCA), 37–43
root certificate, 4, 5
Root Store, 32
Royal Society, 130
RSA (Rivest-Shamir-Aldeman), 2, 3
Rubicon, 10
Russia, 49, 105–108, 117, 125,
  151, 152
  cyber force groups, 107

hackers, 118
interreference and infiltration, 112
Malware, 143

S

Salvadori, Roy, 37
Sandworm attack, 107
Sanger, David, 86, 107, 142
SARS-CoV-2, 129–135
scanning machines, 8
SEC, 50, 78, 112, 119
Secretary of State, 29
Secure Socket Layer (SSL)
  certificate, 5, 24, 25, 29–31,
    33, 34, 47, 51, 73, 83, 93,
    101, 126, 131, 138, 140, 141,
    153, 156–158
secure websites, 47
SecurID two-factor authentication
  products, 161
self-signing certificates, 112
Senate, 9
Senate Intelligence Committee, 112
Senators' websites, 96
senior intelligence groups, 8
Senior Living serviced
  communities, 53
Senna, Aryton, 38
Server Message Block, 124
Service NSW, 92, 93
service outages, 43, 137, 145, 146
Severe Acute Respiratory Syndrome
  (SARS), 129
Seymour, Donna, 46
SF-86 forms, 45
Shadow Brokers, 124, 125, 151
The Shadow Factory (James
  Bamford), 9
Shadow websites, 17, 76
Shamir, Adi, 2
Shangri-la, 17
shareholders, 119

INDEX

179

Shelby, Carroll, 37
Shetty, B. R., 60–62
Siemens Step 7 PLCs, 23
Signals Directorate (Australia), 13
signals intelligence (SIGINT),
29, 121
Silicon Valley, 109
Silver Lake, 113, 116
Situation Rooms, 8, 164
Sky TV, 38
Smart Cities, 135, 159, 167
Snort, 123
Snowden, Edward, 10, 13, 19,
30–31, 121
Sodinokibi Ransomware, 61
Softbank, 145
SolarWinds, 4, 6, 16, 18, 24, 42, 51, 62,
81, 87, 92, 93, 110, 112–114,
118, 119, 123–125, 133, 135,
138–142, 153, 157, 158,
162, 163
attack, 112
breach, 47–49, 103, 112–120, 126,
158, 161, 164
CEO transition, 113
cyberattack, on agencies, 115
digital certificates, 138
MSP group, 115
SEC filing, 114
Security Advisory, 114
shares, 116
stock, 113, 115, 116
SolarWinds Orion software, 113,
114, 117, 118
SolarWinds Orion Sunburst,
116, 117
SolarWinds Orion Supernova
attack, 118
Sony, 49
sophisticated, 77
sophisticated attacks, 47, 48, 153
sophisticated state-based type cyber
hacks, 91

sophistication, 107
Sorenson, Arne, 53
SPA, 37
spectrometer, 133
spoof BA website, 76
SSH keys, 34, 132, 138
standard digital certificate, 4
Starwood, 54, 55
State Department, 115
State Nations, 126, 152
State Sponsored, 62
Stern, Lord Nick, 130
Steven Spielberg movie, 7
Stewart, Sir Jackie, 37, 38
stock sales, 116
Stonycreek Pennsylvania, 8
STORMBREW, 122
Stratus Networks, 116
Stuxnet, 3, 6, 15, 21–22, 24, 27, 28,
34, 39, 42, 48, 90, 103,
105–106, 112, 120, 124,
126, 141, 155, 163, 166
Subdomain hijacking, 62
SubPrime market, 27, 57
Sunburst, 3, 90, 110, 112, 120, 138,
141, 155, 164, 166
Supervisory and Data Control
Acquisition (SCADA), 106
Suricata, 123
Surtees, Henry, 40
Surtees, John, 40
Swiss Ambassador, 65
Swiss Embassy Cybersecurity, 65
Swiss government, 10–11

T

Tailored Access Operations (TAO),
121–122, 124
Taliban, 8
TalkTalk, 147, 148, 154
Tamene, Yared, 108

INDEX

Tehran, 20
Telco firms, 122
terrorism, 29
terrorist attacks of 9/11, 19, 53, 142
The Terrorist Surveillance Program (TSP), 9
The Onion Router (TOR) connections, 122–123
Thesaurus, 10
Thiel, Peter, 10
third-party supply chains, 17
Thoma Bravo, 113, 116, 119
Thompson, Kevin, 113, 114
Tier one banks, 25
Tillerson, Rex, 152
titanium alloy strip, 41
T-Mobile, 148
Towering Inferno, 7
Transport Layer Security (TLS) certificate, 5, 24, 25, 29–31, 33, 34, 51, 61, 73, 80, 93, 101, 123, 126, 131, 138, 140, 141, 153, 156–158
Travelex, 59–61, 75, 77, 132
Treasury Department, 28
email accounts at, 118
Trump, Donald, 107, 117, 152
websites, 96
TSL digital certificate, 47
TULMIT, 122
TURBULENCE, 122
Turing, Alan, 2, 5
TURMOPIL, 122
Tutte, William, 2, 5
Twin Bridges Motor Hotel, 53
Twitter, 124

U

UAE Exchange, 60
UHNJ, 86
UK Agency, 50
UKDPA, 79, 146
UKDPS, 163
Ukraine, 106, 151
Ukraine–Russian tensions, 57
Ukrainian power grid, 106
unemployment in the US, 27
Union Jack, 39
United Nations Security Council, 20
United States Computer Emergency Readiness Team (US-CERT), 46
uranium, 20, 21
uranium-235, 21
uranium-238, 21
uranium oxide, 21
US Agencies, 28
USB stick, 22
US Central Voting system, 34, 165
US cybersecurity policy, 117
US cyberwar fighters, 105
US department of Homeland Security, 108
US Federal Communications Commission (FCC), 53
US General Accounting Office, 49
US Intelligence agencies, 7, 22, 23, 111, 112
US intelligence community, 108
USIS, 45
US legislators Intelligence community, 107
US National Intelligence Estimate (NIE), 20
US Presidents' websites, 96
US Treasury, 118

V

The Vacation Club International, 53
Vatican, 86–88, 152
VAT refunds, 59
Virtual Private Network (VPN), 61

INDEX

VMware, 117
Vote.gov system, 94, 154
vulnerabilities, 18, 61–63, 112, 134

W

The Wall Street Journal, 46
WannaCry Ransomware attack, 120, 124
War on Terrorism, 8, 9
warrantless surveillance controversies, 9
The Washington Post, 10, 13, 116, 125
Webchecker, 154
Weiss, Joe, 15
Westech International, 94, 99
Whitehorn, 31
White House meetings, 17, 21, 116
Whitethorn, 31–35, 65–72, 90, 102, 125–127, 132, 137, 156
Whitethorn Shield, 34, 55, 66, 78, 86, 90, 138
Wi-Fi monitoring system, 53–54
Wild West, 46

William Tutte, 30
World Health Organisation (WHO), 129
World Trade Centres, 7–8
World War II, 30
Worm, 77
would-be attacker, 15

X

Xcel Energy, 16
XKEYSCORE program, 13, 29, 122
Xtreme Rat, 55, 69

Y

Yu Pingan, 46

Z

Zero Days, 22–25, 72, 74, 111, 120, 121, 124, 141, 155
Zero Trust, 166
Zuckerberg, Mark, 10
Zurich, Mondelez V., 57

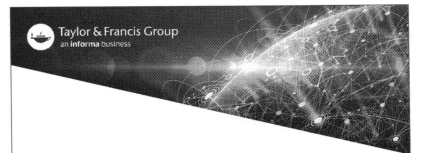

Printed in the United States
by Baker & Taylor Publisher Services